C000256627

Leading Intercessions

Raymond Chapman is Emeritus Professor of English in the University of London and a non-stipendiary priest in the Diocese of Southwark. He is a Vice-Chairman of the Prayer Book Society and is the author of numerous literary and religious titles.

Other books by Raymond Chapman available from the Canterbury Press:

Days of Grace: A Forty-Day Journey with Jesus
A Pastoral Prayer Book: Prayers and Readings for Times of Change, Concern and Celebration
Rhythms of Prayer: A Round the Year Prayer Guide
Stations of the Nativity: Meditations on the Incarnation of Christ
Stations of the Resurrection: Meditations on the Fourteen Resurrection Appearances

Forthcoming:

Following the Gospel through the Year: Reflections on the Gospels for Sundays and Holy Days, Years A, B and C (November 2001)
Godly and Righteous, Peevish and Perverse – Clerics, Nuns and Monks: A Literary Anthology (November 2002)

Leading Intercessions

Prayers for Sundays, Holy Days
and Festivals – Years A, B and C

RAYMOND CHAPMAN

CANTERBURY
PRESS
Norwich

© Raymond Chapman 1997 and 2000

First published 1997 by The Canterbury Press Norwich
(a publishing imprint of Hymns Ancient & Modern Limited
a registered charity)
St Mary's Works, St Mary's Plain,
Norwich, Norfolk NR3 3BH

This edition published 2000
Reprinted 2001

British Library Cataloguing in Publication Data

A catalogue record for this book is available
from the British Library

ISBN 1–85311–377–8 (cased)
1–85311–419–7 (paper)

*Typeset at Rowland Phototypesetting Ltd
Bury St Edmunds, Suffolk
Printed in Great Britain by St Edmundsbury Press Ltd
Bury St Edmunds, Suffolk*

Contents

About the Author

Raymond Chapman is Emeritus Professor of English in the University of London and a non-stipendiary priest in the Diocese of Southwark. He is a Vice-Chairman of the Prayer Book Society and is the author of numerous literary and religious titles.

Books by Raymond Chapman available from The Canterbury Press:

A PASTORAL PRAYER BOOK
Prayers and Readings for Times of Change,
Concern and Celebration

RHYTHMS OF PRAYER
A round the year prayer guide

STATIONS OF THE NATIVITY
Meditations on the Incarnation of Christ

STATIONS OF THE RESURRECTION
Meditations on the fourteen resurrection
appearances

DAYS OF GRACE
A forty-day journey with Jesus

Preface to the Revised Edition

With the publication of *Common Worship*, I have taken the opportunity to revise and expand these prayers for the time of intercession at the Eucharist. A brief invitation to prayer, based on the Gospel for the day, is now provided for each Sunday of the three-year cycle and for Holy Days and Special Occasions. There are also sentences to conclude the intercessions, gathering the petitions together and offering them on behalf of the whole congregation. These introductions and conclusions may suitably be said either by the President or by the person leading the intercessions.

A number of changes have been made in the wording of the intercessions, although their substance is unchanged. It is hoped that these amendments have improved clarity and meaning, and also in some places made for more ease and euphony in speaking.

The suggested headings of subjects for intercession preserves the fivefold order which has come to be commonly used. There may be occasions when this could usefully be changed: for example, at times of national or international crisis, priority might be given to prayers for the world. Any rigid distinction between the Church and the world is to be avoided. Prayers for the departed are now designated as for the Communion of Saints, a reminder of the wholeness of the Christian Church both Militant and Triumphant.

The Notes to the Order for Holy Communion in *Common Worship* specifically permit the use of 'other suitable forms' for intercession, which 'need not always conform to the sequence indicated'.

I am grateful for many appreciative responses to the original book and for helpful suggestions, some of which have been incorporated in this new edition. I particularly thank Christine Smith of The Canterbury Press, who has guided both editions from inception to publication.

Introduction

The structure of this book

These prayers are designed for use with the Revised Common Lectionary which has been adopted by the Church of England, the Scottish Episcopal Church, the Church in Wales and a number of other Churches in the Anglican Communion. It is close to the lectionary currently used by the Roman Catholic Church and is likely to be the preferred lectionary of many other Churches. This is a three-year cycle, drawing on a wide range through the Old and New Testaments and offering more variety than the orders that have generally been used in the past.

The intercessions offered here are based on the Sunday readings for the Principal Service in each year, and on those for other festivals and special occasions. The new lectionary is not so rigidly thematic as the one designed for the Alternative Service Book. Preachers and intercessors will be able to draw their themes from the readings themselves, rather than being theme-directed on every Sunday. The scriptural passages in each case form connections which will suggest a relevant approach, and these connections have been picked up in the words of the intercessions. Since the lectionary is spread over three years, it allows for more continuous readings which follow a book of the Bible over several weeks, and this is especially notable in the Gospels.

Subjects have been drawn mainly from the New Testament readings, with reference to the Old Testament passage when there is only one on offer. Intercessions for major Festivals such as Christmas and Easter which have the same reading in each year, or which clearly create their own themes, are not repeated; otherwise there is something for every Sunday in each of the three years.

As well as the Sunday cycle, there is the cycle of holy days recurring through each year. Most often these will fall on a weekday when there is less likely to be a call for full intercessions, but it is increasingly common to celebrate the most important, especially in the case of a patronal festival, on a proximate Sunday. Intercessions are produced for the main categories – Apostles, Evangelists and so on – and for more general use.

There are also readings and associated intercessions for special occasions. For example, the provision for a service with intention for the Guidance of the Holy Spirit would be appropriate for a Parochial Church Council or similar executive body, and the Unity section for an ecumenical service.

The fivefold division of subjects, which is widely used and has proved valuable in directing attention, is here adopted:

The Church As intercessions are usually offered within an act of public worship, and always on behalf of all Christians, we pray first for the Church as the Body of Christ on earth and for Christ's people in their lives of service.

The world This is the world which God created and Christ came to save. We pray for all human needs and that the lives of people and nations may fulfil the divine purpose.

The community Next we move to the concerns that are most near to us: families, friends, neighbours, those with whom we work. Prayers for the wider world are often necessarily general, but here we can make our requests known more specifically. We pray too for all who live in the area that forms our local community, large or small.

The suffering The compassion of God reaches out to all but is too often blocked by human sin and indifference. Those who suffer are particularly dear to him, and we offer our own sympathy and desire to help those, known or unknown to us, who are afflicted.

The Communion of Saints Prayers for the dead have been part of Christian liturgy from the earliest years. Our remembrance of them draws us into the prayers of the whole Church, seen and unseen, in heaven as well as on earth. We recall our own mortality and affirm our faith in the resurrection to eternal life, and in the fellowship of all Christians, living and departed.

The intercessions can be offered in these sections, within a liturgical structure which invites congregational response, or as a continuous prayer. The breaks between sentences in each section give space for particular desires and concerns to be included, but the prayers can at any point be said without a break. The intercessor will usually wish to mention some specific needs. Clearly, these are suggested words to help intercession and will often benefit from paraphrase or addition. For one example, the word 'community' is often used in the third section and it may be more appropriate to say 'village', 'city', 'school' and so on.

If the custom of the church is to use the second person singular *thou* forms in addressing God, the words can readily be amended. Some care is needed in adapting the verbal forms to correspond. This happens to be the preference of the author of this book, and of many others, but both styles are now current.

Although the collection is envisaged largely for use in an act of public worship, it is hoped that it may be helpful also, for smaller and more informal prayer groups. Further, it is suggested for individual use, to help intercession in personal prayers. Careful reading of the appointed passages of scripture may be followed by meditation and then intercession, not limited by what is here written but perhaps aided by it.

Intercessory prayer

Intercession is only a part of prayer, but it is an important one, and the practice of intercession at the Eucharist is a universal Christian tradition. The Eucharist is principally a service of praise and thanksgiving, culminating in the reception of the sacramental elements of bread and wine. The liturgy also includes instruction, penitence and intercession. Wherever people are moved to pray, it is a basic instinct to ask for blessing and strength in areas of concern. Christians know that in such prayers we are not trying to change the will of God for our own immediate benefit, or to soften the heart of a remote and implacable tyrant.

It is enough to know that it is both our duty and our privilege to bring the needs of individuals and communities before God in prayer. We have the command and example of Christ, and the practice of the Church, to assure us that this is a proper response of faith. It is one of the many ways in which our natural desires are accepted and sanctified. To lift people up in prayer is a token both of our care for them and of our belief in the love of God for all his creatures. In so doing, we are also offering ourselves to be used in the furtherance of what we ask: this is a vital element in intercession, whether individual or on behalf of the whole congregation. As we focus our concerns and make them articulate, we come to realise how much they really mean to us. True intercession is an offering of help as well as a plea for help. It is a recognition that, although God needs nothing from us, he graciously invites and accepts our share in his loving purposes.

The author hopes and prays that this book may indeed be useful to those who are charged with leading intercessions and also to those who wish to widen the intercessory element in their own prayers.

Principal Service

Year A

FIRST SUNDAY OF ADVENT

As we begin to prepare for the coming of the Lord Jesus to share our humanity, let us pray for grace faithfully to acknowledge him as our Saviour and our Judge.

Keep your Church ever watchful, prepared for the call to new service and greater witness ... Give to your faithful people keen eyes and eager minds to know and to perform your will at all times.

Bring to a world absorbed in the present and fearful of the future the vision of a greater glory ... Give wisdom that all work for present needs may be done with the desire that your divine purpose may be fulfilled ... Grant patience to those who must wait to see the results of their work.

May those of our community who have not heard your call to watch and pray be filled with desire to come to your house for worship ... Use us as the means of drawing others into the fellowship of your Kingdom now and to come.

Have mercy on those whose suffering holds them in the agony of the moment ... Bring to them the vision of the time when good shall triumph and there shall be no more pain and sorrow.

We commend into your keeping the souls of those who faithfully looked for the fulfilment of your promise and have entered into the Church Triumphant of the saints . . . Give us grace to hold fast to the same hope of eternal life.

We offer our prayers in the name of the Christ who was long promised, came in humility and will come again in glory.

SECOND SUNDAY OF ADVENT

Having received the revelation of God through his holy word entrusted to human hands, we pray, confident in his care for all people.

As the prophets foretold the coming of Christ, and the Baptist declared his presence, empower your Church to make him known at this present time . . . Guide us with wisdom and understanding in the reading of your word revealed in holy scripture.

Enlighten the people of this world with repentance for past wrong and a new resolve for good . . . Fulfil in our time the promise of peace and reconciliation.

Open our eyes to find your word for us in Bible reading . . . In all our dealings with one another, enable us to speak the truth in love, to be witnesses of faith to all whose lives touch ours.

May the present comfort of your holy word and the hope of future glory bring strength to those who suffer . . . Give them relief through the power of Christ, healing all their ills and making all things new.

Grant that the souls of the departed may share the joy of all who have witnessed to the message of salvation . . . We give thanks for those who have gone before to prepare for us the way of peace.

We offer our words of prayer, that they may be acceptable in the name of the Word made flesh for us.

THIRD SUNDAY OF ADVENT

As the grace of God has opened our way to come before him, let us pray in the assurance that he is present among us.

As the Son of God was made known by mighty works, strengthen his Church in true faith and good deeds . . . Make through her witness a highway to your holiness, a garden in the wilderness.

May the desert places of sin and sorrow blossom as the rose, filled with the joy of your presence . . . Bring light to those who are in darkness, love to the hearts that are barren.

Bless us with your presence in our families and friendships . . . Give us patience in all our dealings with others . . . Where relationships are hurt or broken, give healing and renewal.

As our Lord Jesus performed great wonders of healing, bring relief and renewed health to the sick and injured . . . Have mercy on those who after long illness are despairing of health . . . Give them hope and trust in your unfailing love.

Grant rest to those who have seen the promises fulfilled, all troubles ended, all distresses healed . . . Make them perfect in the peace of Christ.

Seeking to follow the way which the Lord has shown to us, we make our prayers in his Name.

FOURTH SUNDAY OF ADVENT

Let us pray with confidence in the promise that what we ask in the name of our Lord Jesus will be acceptable to our heavenly Father.

Strengthen your Church in the name of Jesus, to know the power of the Saviour, of God with us ... Hold us fast in the obedience and faith that enabled Joseph to perform your will in the work of salvation.

Give hope and assurance to those who bear the burden of authority in difficult times ... May all who are doubtful and anxious know that the promise of salvation is made to all who will receive it.

Help us to be worthy of the name of Jesus which we honour in our faith ... Number us among those who bear the message of salvation, to be a light to those with whom we live and work.

Bring new hope and confidence to all who are in doubt and uncertainty ... Give peace to the troubled minds that distrust those near to them, and bring them new strength in love.

We pray for those who have known and believed the message of salvation and now rejoice in its fulfilment ... Be merciful to those who in this world were doubtful and did not find perfect trust: make them also sharers of the promise.

In humble trust we offer these prayers to Almighty God, through the Name that is above every name.

CHRISTMAS DAY

God sent his Son to live as a man among us: let us pray in the confidence of our new life in him.

Rejoicing in the birth of our Lord and Saviour, we pray that the Church may be continually reborn ... Let us share the humility of the manger, the adoration of the shepherds, and the love of the Holy Family, in the light of him who is the Light of the world.

Pity and pardon this world of conflict, deaf to the message of peace ... Bring harmony where there is strife between nations and where people are divided by suspicion and bitterness ... Heal those who have no peace within themselves.

We pray for the families and friends with whom we celebrate this happy time ... Give us true love, unselfish desires and grateful hearts ... We pray especially for the children, for their unclouded joy at this time ... Create in us a pattern of human love that will lead them to the love of God who sent his Son as a little child.

We pray for those who cannot feel the joy of Christmas, through the burden of sickness, bereavement or other distress ... Comfort with your presence all who are separated at this time from those they love ... Bring the light of Christ into their afflicted lives.

Have mercy on the departed who, having shared with Christ their human birth and infancy, have shared with him also the death of the body ... Make their joy complete, in the Kingdom where there is neither birth nor death but abundant life without end.

Through Christ who is the hope of the nations and the joy of all people we make our prayers to God who is most wonderfully with us.

FIRST SUNDAY OF CHRISTMAS

Let us pray, with joy for humanity redeemed and in sorrow for humanity still marred by sin.

As we rejoice in the Incarnation of Jesus, we acknowledge also his suffering for our salvation ... Give to the Church grace to proclaim both the joy and the great price of God's love.

May the message of this holy time be heard in a world where mistrust and cruelty still bring the abuse of power . . . Give understanding to those whose indifference wounds the divine heart of love.

In the strength of the incarnate Christ make us instruments of his peace . . . Reconcile us where we are in dispute with others and cleanse us from all resentment.

We bring before you the innocent who suffer by human sin . . . We pray for civilians caught up in war, for victims of terrorism and crime, for children abused: protect them with your power of love.

We remember those who died in childhood or youth . . . As they find their fulfilment in the life eternal, comfort those who remain to mourn for them.

In our fellowship with all God's people, worshipping here on earth or in the fullness of his glory, we offer these our prayers.

SECOND SUNDAY OF CHRISTMAS

Let us pray in the unity of all who worship Jesus Christ, the Prince of Peace and the Lord of mercy.

You have gathered your people together, with the purpose that they may be one . . . Bring to the Church the complete unity that is your will . . . Give us grace to proclaim the promises prepared from the beginning and revealed in Jesus Christ.

In a world torn apart by divisions and strife, lead us back into the way of peace, heal what is damaged and unite what is sundered . . . Give to all in authority wisdom and a true desire for peace.

Bless our families with the sharing of love . . . Help us to live in peace and harmony with our neighbours

. . . We have seen the light of Christ: let it shine through us.

Have mercy on those who are broken in body, mind or spirit . . . Come to those who are torn apart by anxiety and give them the confidence of knowing your loving purpose.

As we remember those who are now gathered into unity with you, made whole in your presence, we offer our imperfect faith that we too may come to the perfection of eternal life.

May our prayers be joined with the worship of saints and angels, and may we too be messengers of God's peace.

THE EPIPHANY

Let us pray in the glorious light of Christ who leads his people in all their worship and adoration.

As the Wise Men were led to worship the infant Jesus, so lead your Church to know you more clearly and to do your work on earth more faithfully . . . Give us deeper reverence in worship, humbly to adore the mystery of the Incarnation.

Guide those with authority and influence to acknowledge the lordship of Christ . . . Teach those who control the resources of the world to use them responsibly . . . Turn the hearts of those who work only for their own interests and bring them to love others in the freedom of your service.

Help those who work in our local community, and those with whom we work, to offer their gifts and talents for the good of all . . . Make us witnesses to your truth through the quiet offering of our lives.

Bring reconciliation to families broken by infidelity and misunderstanding ... Have mercy on orphaned and neglected children ... Visit and relieve the homeless and those driven out by war or persecution.

We pray for those who have died in childhood, that their lives may be fulfilled in eternal life ... Comfort those who mourn for them with the knowledge that they are free from all suffering and are close to you for ever.

May our offerings of prayer be acceptable to the King of glory, revealed to all who seek him diligently in faith.

THE BAPTISM OF CHRIST (FIRST SUNDAY OF EPIPHANY)

In obedience to the Lord who for our sake was obedient to the human condition and gave us the example of holy baptism, we offer our prayers.

As Christians are united in baptism, break down the barriers that keep us apart ... All things are made new in Jesus your Son: renew your Church, appointed to make him known to all nations.

Open the eyes that are blind with false values, liberate those who are held in the prison of their sins, lighten the darkness of ignorance and error, that the world may be truly free.

Fill us with the love of Jesus, revealed to us in faith ... As our lives touch other lives, make us agents of the good news that he is our Saviour.

Look with pity on those whose lives are bruised, whose hopes are quenched ... Give them new life through the Holy Spirit who descended on Jesus, the beloved, in his baptism.

We commend to your love those who, washed in the water of baptism, were close to you in this life and now are closer in the life eternal ... By your grace, may we and they be one in you.

Being washed with the water of repentance and new life, we pray as members through hope of the Kingdom of God.

SECOND SUNDAY OF EPIPHANY

We who are disciples of Christ in our time join in prayer for his Church, and for all people.

As you have called us to your service, make us worthy of our calling ... Your loving purpose was before all ages; let it not fail through those who are your Church in this generation.

Come with your powerful love to those who have not heard your call or have failed to answer it ... Draw the mighty and the humble of the world to follow where Jesus has led.

May our homes be radiant with your presence through our love and hospitality to others ... Help us to do our daily work knowing that it is part of our calling to be your disciples.

Give to the suffering the comfort of your presence ... Make the lives of the poor rich, as the disciples were made rich through their calling.

We give thanks for those whose faith was confirmed to the end, who were called to be saints not by any merit of their own but by your grace ... May they be joyful in the life that was prepared for them from the beginning.

May Almighty God, who shows the way to men and women who have heard his voice, graciously hear us when we raise our own voices in prayer.

THIRD SUNDAY OF EPIPHANY

Guided by the great light of divine glory, let us pray to God who calls us to follow and worship him.

Illumine the Church with the light of your truth ... Keep her faithful to her one Lord, Jesus Christ, avoiding contention and never trusting in human strength alone.

Shine with divine love on those who walk in darkness ... Let the nations hear the gentle voice of your call and respond with joy, that there may be peace in place of strife.

As the disciples were called to be fishers of people for the Kingdom, make us obedient to the call to be ministers of the Gospel in our homes, our work, our community.

As our Lord Jesus in his earthly ministry healed all kinds of sickness and disease, may his healing power come now to the sick and injured ... Strengthen and enable all who work to heal the sick.

We remember before you those who were your disciples in this world and now rejoice in the great light of heaven ... We give thanks that you have indeed multiplied their joy.

Rejoicing that we are led in the way of obedience and love, we pray to the Lord of light and truth.

FOURTH SUNDAY OF EPIPHANY

Let us pray to God, our gracious host and divine guest, giver of all good gifts.

Loving God, whose foolishness is greater than human wisdom, strengthen your Church to proclaim the faith of Christ crucified ... Let no contempt or opposition hold her back from her duty to the world.

Have mercy on a world made foolish by misuse of knowledge and power ... Grant to those who think themselves wise the simple trust that is the only hope of humanity. Where there are families in need, bring comfort ... Where there is joy, give blessing ... May the presence of Jesus protect and sanctify all marriages.

As the daily miracle of your creation brings food and drink for human needs, have mercy on the hungry of the world ... Give us eager hearts and ready hands to give relief.

We commend to your love those who trusted in the Cross and now are called to the great feast where the faithful departed rejoice in the fullness of the divine love.

May the Lord who most bountifully answers every need hear us as we call upon him in our prayers.

THE PRESENTATION OF CHRIST

With confidence in the divine light revealed to our human race, let us pray to the Lord.

We give thanks for knowledge of our salvation, seen with the eye not of sight but of faith ... Enlighten the Church to be a true Temple to the glory of Christ and a witness to the world.

Make the divine light to shine on all nations ...
Through Christ, who took our nature fully upon him,
deliver your people from all evil.

In our families and friendships, make us a light to
lighten the lives of others ... Come with the healing
fire of your love to cleanse all that is not right in our
community, that all may know their true Redeemer.

Bless and protect the vulnerable ones of our common
humanity: the babies, the parents who have few of
the world's goods, the aged and infirm ... Be their
strong defence in times of need and keep them from
harm.

We pray for those who have departed in peace and
come into the glorious light of eternity ... Receive
them into the salvation that was prepared for them
from the beginning.

We end our prayers in the peace of God who has given
us his Son to be the Saviour of the world.

ORDINARY TIME

PROPER 1

Let us pray, as those who seek to be faithful members
of the Kingdom of Heaven.

Keep the Church steadfast in the way of your commandments ... Make your people a light to their generation, faithful to the Gospel of love.

Guide all people into the mystery that challenges the
wisdom of the world ... Show the way of true repentance which does not rest on outward signs but turns
back sincerely to obey your will.

Inspire us with your love, to bring light to those with whom we live and work ... Open our eyes to see where there is need for relief to the hungry body or the clouded mind.

Have compassion on those who are afraid, who feel inadequate for the demands of life ... Grant them confidence in the hidden wisdom of your word.

We give thanks for those who have been faithful to your law and shone as lights in their earthly lives ... Grant them the fullness of your presence, where true wisdom is revealed.

Honouring the Law of God and seeking true righteousness, we make our prayers to fulfil his commandments.

PROPER 2

With purity of heart and in love to all his people, let us pray to the Lord.

Guide your Church to walk in the right way, holding faith in Christ alone ... Working together for your will, may we be truly of your building.

When so many conflicting voices are heard and burdens of choice are often heavy, lead the peoples of the world into the right way, to follow life and not death, good and not evil.

Inspire us, our families and friends, with the spirit of true love and purity ... Take away the hidden anger and the unresolved conflicts that can mar our lives.

Have mercy on those whose anger and resentment holds them back from fullness of life ... Help those who are hurt and cannot forgive ... Heal the wounds of broken faith in close relationships.

We give thanks for the faith of those who have laboured well in this world and are now at rest ... We pray for those who died bitter and unforgiving: grant them pardon and peace.

Submitting to the judgement of the only true Judge and trusting in his mercy, we lay before him this our offering of prayer.

PROPER 3

Let us pray, in love for God our only strength, and for all his people. .

Strengthen your Church, established on the firm foundation of Christ ... Make her holy in all her works, seeking always the way of righteousness.

Arouse your divine compassion in the hearts of all people ... Inspire in us generosity to the poor and neglected, reconciliation and trust between enemies.

Make us loving towards our neighbours, finding in each the image of Christ ... Forgive us our thoughts of hostility and failures of love, and make us eager to forgive others.

Come and relieve those who suffer through the anger of the unforgiving ... Those who are in want through the greed of the selfish ... Those who are held in the power of their own bitterness.

Grant rest to the souls who in this life made Christ their one foundation ... Hold them in the peace of wrongs forgiven and enmities overcome.

Through him on whom all our hope is founded, Christ the support and strength of the faithful, we offer our prayers.

SECOND SUNDAY BEFORE LENT

Let us pray to God, our creator, sustainer and redeemer, for our needs and the needs of the whole world.

Fill the Church, your new creation, with the spirit of hope ... Enable her to proclaim to all people the good news of the Kingdom and its righteousness.

Restore to a world created holy and beautiful but which we have defaced by indifference and greed, the reverence due to all your creatures ... Give hope and trust to take away the anxiety for the future that troubles so many.

Bring to all who are of our community the assurance that they are your children and that you will meet their needs ... Let our own trust be a witness to others.

Have mercy on those whose troubles hold them back from knowing the beauty of the world ... Deliver them from fear and show them the joy of your salvation.

We commend those who have been delivered from the cares of this transitory life ... Hold them in the life of the Kingdom where lost beauty is restored and lost innocence is renewed.

Trusting in the unfailing love of God for all that he has made, we offer our prayer and praise before him.

SUNDAY NEXT BEFORE LENT

Let us pray in obedience to God's holy law and in adoration of his glory revealed in his Son.

As we have received your commandments, give to your Church a prophetic voice to declare them, that

the glory of Christ may shine in all people ... Give us
the light that we cannot find without your guidance.

Look with pity on a world lacking direction and purpose ... Lighten the nations with the vision of truth
revealed of old in your holy mountain.

Grant to us, and to our families and friends, the desire
to draw closer to Christ and to live our lives with him
... Speak to us through the Holy Spirit as you spoke
to the prophets and apostles.

Send the light of Christ into the darkness of those who
are in need and distress at this time ... Give them the
assurance of salvation.

We give thanks that the faithful departed are trans-
figured in the light of your love ... Give us grace to
live according to your commandments and to follow
in their steps.

May these our prayers be found worthy in the light
of Christ, our guide in all our words and ways.

ASH WEDNESDAY

In penitence and faith seeking the path of holiness, let
us pray to the Lord.

Inspire your Church to witness to her Lord at this
season by following him in humility and simplicity of
life ... Give us wisdom to make good resolves and
grace to maintain them ... Grant that we may so
deepen and purify our worship that we shall know
more fully your holy will.

We pray for those who use the good things of this
world selfishly and for those whose power makes
them insensitive to the needs of others ... Show them
the way of love and self-denial ... Cleanse the peoples

of the earth from worshipping the false gods of wealth and possessions.

Fill us with the grace of prayer and service . . . Enable us to give ourselves more readily, in our homes, our work and all our dealings with others . . . Shield those known to us who are beset by temptation to do wrong.

We pray for those whose lives are austere not by choice but by misfortune . . . For those who have no comforts to renounce because they struggle to survive . . . We pray for the starving and undernourished, the homeless and the unprotected.

Have mercy on the dead who once trusted in the things of this world . . . Have mercy on those who looked for salvation through their own deeds . . . In your unfailing love, grant them the eternal life which all may gain through faith but none can merit.

Sorrowful for our sins and joyful for the means of pardon, we begin our Lenten pilgrimage in prayer.

FIRST SUNDAY OF LENT

Let us pray to the Lord who guides us through the wilderness of temptation into our fellowship with him and with one another.

Forgive the weakness and failures of those who call themselves followers of Christ . . . By his victory over temptation, strengthen your Church in his service.

Have mercy on a fallen world, disobedient to your law . . . Restore in all our humanity your image that has been defaced through sin . . . Inspire those in authority with more concern for the care of natural things.

Make us more aware of the beauty of creation in the places where we live and work . . . Give us grace to resist the temptation to use your creatures for our own pleasure.

Have mercy on those who have fallen deeply into sin and despair ... Lead them into the new life which Christ has opened to all who will believe.

We commend to your mercy the souls of those who have passed from the temptations of this world ... Forgive their sins and receive them into the perfection of your new creation.

Beset by temptation but trusting in the power of Christ alone to save, we commend ourselves to his mercy through our prayers.

SECOND SUNDAY OF LENT

Let us pray in the power of the Holy Spirit who guides and enables the people of God.

As your word has been revealed from the days of Abraham until this time, make us faithful in our generation to believe your promises and follow the guidance of your Holy Spirit.

Open the ears of a world that seems deaf to your word ... Grant that the lives that have fallen aside from the true way may be born again.

Keep us, our families and friends, alert to your calling ... As we come to you in questioning, relieve our doubts and fears ... Breathe new life into our homes and the places where we work.

Give courage to those who are fearful of what lies before them, who face the call to depart into new and unknown ways ... Keep them steadfast in hope and trust.

Grant to the faithful departed the eternal life promised by our Lord Jesus ... Unite our prayers with them and with those who have believed your word through all the ages.

May the Holy Spirit direct and sanctify these our prayers and lead us in the way of truth.

THIRD SUNDAY OF LENT

That we may worship in spirit and in truth, let us pray with reverence to Almighty God.

Source of the living water, forgive us when we fail in trust and serenity towards you ... Through all times of trouble and difficulty, keep your Church constant to worship you in spirit and in truth.

Come to a world that is thirsty for peace and security ... Calm the restlessness of humanity with the knowledge of salvation won by Jesus Christ.

We pray for those known to us who are suffering in their marriages or other close relationships ... We remember also those who know you imperfectly, and pray that they may understand and be made whole.

Look with compassion on those who know too well the pains of bodily thirst ... Strike through the hardness of our hearts, that we may work for relief in areas of drought and famine.

With confidence in the love of Christ who died for sinners, we commend the souls departed this life ... We give thanks for the eternal life in which none shall ever thirst again.

We offer these prayers to God who knows the secrets of all hearts and gives us the water of life.

FOURTH SUNDAY OF LENT

Let us pray for the light of Christ, that we may worship with a clear vision of his love.

Open the eyes of your people, to have a right judgement in all things by the light of your truth . . . Shield us from the works of darkness that may threaten the purity of your Church.

When so many cannot see their way and fall into indifference or despair, grant that the light of the Gospel may be known to all nations . . . Give true discernment to those who go astray through the false judgement of outward sight.

Be close to our families and save them from all that would offend against you . . . Bring the brightness of your presence into our community, to reveal and correct those things which are contrary to your will.

Have mercy on the blind and weak of sight . . . Guide those who seek to relieve them, and increase our will to help where resources are needed.

We remember those whose eyes are open indeed as they live in the fullness of your glory . . . We give thanks for the way of salvation shown by Christ, the Light of the world.

That we may have the perfect vision of faith, may these our prayers lead us to closer knowledge of God.

or **MOTHERING SUNDAY** see p. 158

FIFTH SUNDAY OF LENT

Let us pray to God, the giver of life in this world and in his eternal Kingdom.

Breathe new life into the Church ... Break through our sloth and indifference ... Give us power to proclaim Jesus as the Resurrection and the life.

Bless the wilderness places of the world, where the springs of hope have become dry ... Heal with your life-giving Spirit all who are weighed down by the burden of materialism.

Lead us, our families and friends, in the way of true righteousness ... Give us lives more joyful in the assurance of sins forgiven.

Comfort those who mourn, so that they may know that death is not the end ... Give the Spirit of life to those whose spirits are broken by sorrow.

Confident in the promise that those who believe in Jesus Christ will live though they are dead, we give thanks for all who have left their earthly body and entered into the greater life of the Spirit.

We make our prayers in the name of Christ who has raised us from the death of sin to eternal life.

PALM SUNDAY

Let us follow in the way of Christ and pray through him to the Father.

Give true humility to your people, making them more worthy to proclaim the sufferings of Christ, the just for the unjust ... As he was smitten for us, strengthen us when we must bear scorn and opposition for his sake.

Turn and soften those who take the false and easy way when choice is demanded ... Cleanse the world of corruption that is concealed under a show of goodness.

Give us the desire to serve those whose lives touch our own ... Let us honour one another for the sake of him who humbled himself to the Cross for us.

Have compassion on those who are condemned by unjust laws and cruel regimes ... May they feel, in their suffering, the suffering love of Christ.

We pray for those who have been put to death through anger, blindness or cowardice or by the violence of injustice ... Give them the peace that was refused them in this life.

Casting our cares and our sins before the feet of Christ, may we have grace to follow him to the end.

MAUNDY THURSDAY

Let us pray, in the joy of the Lord's sacrament and in the sorrow of his Passion.

Inspire the Church with the presence of Jesus Christ, here with us as he was with his disciples on the eve of his Passion ... Draw us closer to you and to one another in the celebration of holy communion.

Recalling your great acts of mercy, we pray for the world, for freedom from the slavery of injustice and oppression, and all that holds people back from fullness of life.

As you gave to your disciples a new commandment of love, give the spirit of love to all among whom we live ... Let the healing power of our communion spread beyond these walls, to make many whole.

Have mercy on those who have not learned to love ... Grant that those who feel themselves to be without value may be confident of their worth shown in Christ's saving death.

We pray for those who in this world followed Christ and died in the assurance of his love . . . May the grace of his communion fortify us until we rest with them.

As we come to the Table of the Lord, may these our prayers be united with the great Prayer of Thanksgiving.

GOOD FRIDAY

In sorrow, in penitence and in thanksgiving for the divine sacrifice of the Passion, let us pray.

Give to your Church grace to enter deeply into the sad mystery of this day . . . As we stand before the Cross of Jesus Christ, make us more worthy to take that Cross as the sign of our faith.

Have mercy on a world that goes its way ignorant or forgetful of Christ's sacrificial love . . . In the power of the Cross, let his true kingship be established.

As Jesus cared for his mother and his friend even in the hour of death, let nothing diminish our concern for one another . . . As he was crucified near to a city, may his saving love come into our homes.

Look with compassion on all who are bruised and smitten by suffering . . . In the sufferings of Christ, let them find healing.

We pray for all whose earthly lives have ended . . . We pray that the death which destroyed death shall be their life.

Now and at all times, we offer our prayers through Jesus Christ, crucified for us.

EASTER EVE

In quiet confidence and joyful expectation, let us pray to the Lord.

With sorrow and hope we offer our worship this day ... Grant to all the faithful the grace to wait upon your will in peace and stillness.

Bring to busy, restless humanity the blessing of calm ... May the message of hope be preached even in the darkest places of the world.

Bless our families with the peace of Christ ... Heal disputes and divisions in our community with the remembrance that Christ suffered for us all, even to death.

Give rest to the tired minds and bodies of those for whom Christ suffered in the flesh ...

Have mercy on all who mourn, and give them confidence in a new and greater life. Be close to those who sleep now in death ... Come to the dying, and bring them with Jesus through the tomb into eternal life.

Through the peace of trust and repose in Jesus Christ, we offer these our prayers.

EASTER DAY

Let us pray to the Father who raised his Son to life that we might live for ever in him.

Strengthen your Church to be the Body of Christ at work in the world ... Heal our divisions and imperfections, make whole this visible body so that it may truly reflect his glorious Body ... Give grace to ministers of the Gospel in proclaiming the message of the Resurrection.

We pray that the joy of the Resurrection may be known throughout the world, that those who are ignorant of the love of Christ may feel his presence and share his risen life ... May all human endeavour become part of the new creation and the life without end.

Give grace this Easter time to heal the wounds of differences among our families, friends and neighbours ... By the offering and acceptance of pardon where there has been wrong, may we know together the fullness of the Easter life.

Grant to all who suffer the knowledge of where true healing is to be found ... Heal the hurt and broken bodies, give peace to the troubled minds, restore hope to the grieved and anxious spirits ... Lead all human sorrow through the pain of the dying Christ to the joy of his Resurrection.

As we rejoice in the Resurrection of Christ our Saviour, we pray for all who, like him, have suffered the death of the body ... We pray that the power which brought him from the grave may give them a part in his victory over death and in his risen life for ever.

Risen with Christ and filled with new life, we pray as his people on earth.

SECOND SUNDAY OF EASTER

Let us pray, in the peace of the risen Christ and with the faith of the Apostles.

As the Apostles proclaimed the good news of the Resurrection, inspire the Church to make it known to all people ... Come with power among us and confirm our faith.

Break through the barriers that close human hearts against your love ... Let all people understand their true inheritance through grace.

Make us your witnesses to others, bringing news of the Risen Christ to our families and friends, our neighbours and colleagues ... May the peace of your presence spread through our community.

Have mercy on those who cannot grasp the reality of your love for them ... Give confidence to those who are constrained by doubt and fear.

We give thanks for those who held their faith through the trials of this world and have received their salvation, resting in the peace where all wounds are healed, all doubts dispelled.

May God pardon our doubts and imperfections in these and all our prayers.

THIRD SUNDAY OF EASTER

Let us pray to the Father through the Son who is close to us now and always.

As the risen Christ was made known in the breaking of bread, give grace to all Christian people through the holy communion of his Body and Blood ... Forgive our failures of devotion when we come to his Table.

Open the eyes of those who do not understand that Christ is near to them ... May the truth of his sacrifice for men and women everywhere be known in all the world.

Guide us to discern Christ in all our lives, in our friends and colleagues, in those that we find difficult to love ... Inspire us to share the good news of the Resurrection.

Have mercy on those who are so cast down by sorrow that they cannot feel the divine love ... Lighten their darkness with the light of the new life in Christ.

Abide with those whose days on earth are spent and who now rest in Christ ... Grant to all who have walked with him the fullness of his presence.

That our eyes may be opened and our hearts warmed with faith, we offer our prayers.

FOURTH SUNDAY OF EASTER

Let us pray to the Lord, by whose grace we are led in the paths of righteousness.

Strengthen your Church in the desire for true fellowship ... Make us one in heart and mind, so that we may share the riches of your grace with all.

Make all the world hear the voice of the Good Shepherd and turn from the ways of evil ... Give strength to those who work for better sharing of this world's goods.

Enfold our homes and places of work in the love of Christ ... Let nothing destroy our care for one another.

Have mercy on all who like sheep have gone astray ... Lead them back to the true fold of your love where they may find fullness of life.

We remember those who have passed through the door of death and found it the door of life prepared by the Resurrection of Christ ... Grant them eternal life.

We offer our prayers in the name of Jesus Christ, the great Shepherd of his sheep.

FIFTH SUNDAY OF EASTER

In the faith of Christ, we pray as he has commanded us and given us his example.

As we have become your people by grace, make us more worthy of our calling ... Lead your Church to follow Jesus in all things as the way, the truth and the life.

Spread your healing presence in a world where many cannot bear to hear the truth ... Give grace and power to those who seek to do great works in the name of Christ.

Use us as living stones to build a community in your name ... Keep us, our families and friends, in the true way.

Soothe the hearts that are troubled and guide the feet that do not know the way ... Grant, to all who suffer, the vision of Christ risen and glorified, at the right hand of the Father.

May the Lord who has gone before to prepare a place for us, receive the souls of the faithful and grant them the perfect knowledge of his love.

We pray in the name of the Son, in whom the Father is revealed and glorified.

SIXTH SUNDAY OF EASTER

Let us pray in the Spirit who gives us the means and the grace to pray.

As we profess our love, inspire us to give proof of love by keeping your commandments ... Grant that the Church may be always guided by the Spirit of truth. *C o P*

As you have created all things, and made our whole human race of one blood, bring harmony and peace to the peoples of the world ... Dispel the darkness of ignorance, that all may fully know you and worthily worship you. *C o P*

Unite in love the members of our local community ... Let the Holy Spirit dwell in our homes and give us peace.

Set free all who are held in ignorance and superstition ... Bring into true faith those whose desire for forbidden knowledge has led them into evil ways. *— Sick*

As Christ came after his Passion to release the departed souls, so may his presence always bring comfort to the dying and eternal life to those who have died.

Rejoicing that we live in the ever-living Christ, we pray in his name.

ASCENSION DAY

With hearts and minds lifted to Christ who has ascended on high, let us pray.

As we join with all Christian people in giving praise for the Ascension of our Lord Jesus Christ, we pray for the Church that he left to continue his work on earth ... Faithful to her calling, may she witness to his glory by declaring and practising his saving love.

We pray that through the glorified humanity of Jesus all people may be brought to a better understanding of our human nature ... By your power, renew this world that is upheld in your love ... Teach all to respect the dignity and rights of others as children of one Father.

Grant that in our daily lives our vision may not be limited by present concerns ... May all that we do, in our families and in our work, be seen in the light of Christ and offered to him as the Master of all our service.

Have mercy on all who suffer in body or mind ... Give them strength and hope in the Ascended Christ ... May his passage from suffering to glory lift them out of their troubles into new life.

We pray for all who have gone where Christ has led, whose human nature has been transformed in his presence ... Teach us to be ready to follow them, confident in his love and guided by his example.

We offer these prayers through the divine power of Christ, shed abroad in all the world.

SEVENTH SUNDAY OF EASTER

Let us pray to the Father, glorified in the Son to whom all things in heaven and earth are given.

May all Christian people be one in the glory of Christ ... Bless evangelists and preachers, that your Church may make the faith known to all nations.

Draw the races and nations of the world together in better understanding ... Break down the barriers of hostility and ignorance that hold your children apart.

Make us bearers of your word to those among whom we live ... May we be sensitive to discern and heal the misunderstandings that cause division.

Comfort and relieve those who suffer for their faith . . .
Protect your chosen ones who are rejected by the world.

Grant to the departed the eternal life in which is true
knowledge of God in Christ . . . May they for ever
share in his glory.

We pray through Jesus Christ, who has called us to
the true knowledge of God.

PENTECOST

In the power of the Holy Spirit that we have received
by grace, let us pray.

Grant to the Church strength, wisdom and judgement
through the Holy Spirit . . . Release in your people the
power of a living witness to the whole world, fulfilling
your command to those who seek to follow you in
truth.

Have mercy on a world where there is often speech
without communication, relationships without love,
and where people are separated by barriers of race
and nationality . . . Send your Holy Spirit to show
men and women their true needs and teach them to
live together without fear.

Grant us right judgement in our families, friendships
and work . . . May we know your presence in every
situation . . . Give us grace to reflect your love in our
care for those with whom we share our lives.

Break through the darkness of unhappy lives with the
light of your healing and guidance . . . Have mercy on
those who have never known you . . . Redeem and
restore those who have lost the faith they once had.

We pray for those who now rejoice in the perfect
knowledge and unclouded vision of your nearer

DEPARTED

presence ... May we who know and worship you imperfectly here come at last into that same eternal light.

May our prayers be worthy to stand in the pure light of the Holy Spirit.

ORDINARY TIME

TRINITY SUNDAY

Let us pray with faith to the blessed and glorious Trinity, Father, Son and Holy Spirit.

Preserve your Church in the true faith, to acknowledge with awe and reverence the mystery of the Holy Trinity ... Fill our worship with adoration ... Give us due humility and assurance as members of the Church which you have created, loved and sanctified.

Open human eyes to the wonder of things unseen ... Make all lives richer in the hope of blessings more than we can comprehend ... Give clearer vision to those in positions of power and influence.

Grant to us in our own lives a share in the mutual love of the Holy Trinity ... May that unbroken harmony be shown in our families, in our work and in all our relationships.

Have mercy on those whose lives are crippled by strain and anxiety in themselves, and hostility to others ... Release their tension, give them inward peace, restore them to the wholeness which is your will for all.

We pray for the departed who in this world held fast to the faith of the Holy Trinity and now adore you for ever ... May their example strengthen and prepare us for the coming of joy made complete and love made perfect in your heavenly Kingdom.

May our prayers be received in the unity of the Holy Trinity, three Persons and one God.

PROPER 4

Let us pray to our heavenly Father, who calls us into his Kingdom.

Strengthen your Church to stand firmly on her divine foundation in Christ . . . May the faith which we profess be shown in works of justice, care and compassion.

Lead all people into the way of truth . . . When choice is demanded, grant true judgement so that the world may grow closer to the way of salvation.

Keep us constant in Christian love for all who come into our lives . . . Show us ways in which we can make our faith a clear sign to others . . . Protect our community from the foolishness that brings destruction.

Have mercy on all who have gone astray and chosen evil ways . . . Give greater assurance to those who are afraid or ashamed to confess their faith.

Receive into your Kingdom the souls of those who have died . . . Redeemed by grace, may they be forgiven for their sins and rest in peace.

Trusting in Jesus Christ, the only sure foundation, we make our prayers in his name.

PROPER 5

Let us pray to God, who hears the prayers of sinners who trust in his mercy.

Confirm the Church as the true heir of the promise
. . . Empower your people to declare in their time your
everlasting love.

Look with pity on a world that is often sick and does
not know its need of healing . . . Lift the crushing weight
of fear from those who live by law without mercy.

Bless our families, friends and neighbours with health
of mind and body . . . Fill us with love and forgiveness
for those who have offended us . . . Help us to receive
them in love, acknowledging our own need of healing
and pardon.

Have pity on those who feel that society has despised
and rejected them . . . Come with your healing power
to the chronically sick who despair of health . . . Make
them know that they are not forsaken in their suffering.

Raise up to eternal life the souls of the departed . . .
Have mercy on all who mourn, especially for the death
of a child.

That we may be made whole through faith in Christ,
we pray in his name.

PROPER 6

Let us pray for the Church entrusted to the Disciples
and the world into which they were sent.

As Jesus called the twelve to be disciples, make all
members of the Church faithful followers in the way
that he taught . . . Strengthen the hope and love that
belong to Christian people.

By the Holy Spirit, bring the radiance of your love
into the hearts of all who do not know you . . . Make

the Gospel known to those who wander as lost sheep in the world.

Open our eyes to recognise the needs of others who come close to us . . . As we go on our way, fill us with desire to speak the good news of the Kingdom.

Relieve and comfort those who suffer from any kind of sickness . . . Empower those who care for them . . . Give new hope to those who have lost it through distress of body or mind.

As the living receive your divine compassion in their suffering, grant mercy to those who have died and gather them into your eternal Kingdom.

Called to labour for the Lord, we pray that all we do and say may be truly in his name.

PROPER 7

That all Christian people may be one and witnesses to the world, let us pray to the Lord.

United by baptism into the death of Christ, we seek to be bearers of his life . . . Give to your faithful people the strength to take up the Cross and follow Christ.

Where selfishness makes people cling to false values, reveal the way of peace through the death of self . . . Give freedom from the sin that diminishes fullness of life.

Bless us, our families, friends and neighbours, with the spirit of mutual care . . . As servants of our Master, let us be servants of one another, unselfish in our relationships, seeking the common good.

Be close to those who are persecuted for their faith . . . Shield them from violence and give them hope.

Enrich with new life those who have died in faith . . .
As they passed through the waters of baptism in
this world, bring them through the gate of death into
glory.

Seeking new life through the saving death of Christ,
we pray in his name.

PROPER 8

Let us pray to the Lord, by whose grace we know that
he is present here with us.

Save us from falling back into the sin from which
we have been made free . . . Shield the Church from
carelessly accepting your grace without remembering
the cost of our salvation.

Hear the cries of the world in the thirst of the body
and the thirst of the soul . . . Open the minds of all to
the message of salvation.

Help us to care for all who are our special responsibility through family or friendship . . . Teach us to receive
your little ones in love, that we may discern the needs
of our community and seek to meet them in the name
of Christ.

Have mercy on all who are held in the slavery of sin
. . . Give to those damaged by addiction to evil habits
the strength that they cannot find in themselves.

We pray that the departed may be released from the
penalty due to sin . . . In your mercy, grant them your
promised gift of eternal life.

We stand in the presence of God, praying that our
faith may be shown in works of love.

PROPER 9

Let us pray through the Son to the Father, Lord of heaven and earth.

Keep the Church strong in the law of Christ, resisting the temptation to accept false values ... May your people in their generation be truly the children of wisdom.

Have pity on a world full of discontent, restless and finding no lasting satisfaction ... Guide into the right way all who desire the good but give way to evil.

Help us to discern and follow the right way in all our relationships ... May the knowledge of your truth be known to this community ... Give wisdom to those who hold responsibility in it and make them agents of your law of love.

Have mercy on those whose lives are weary and whose burdens are heavy ... May they come to know the freedom of trust in Jesus Christ.

We pray for those who have been delivered from their mortal bodies ... Now that the struggle with sin is over, receive them into your presence.

Secure in the rest that Christ has given, we pray in his name.

PROPER 10

Let us pray to God, through whose word our words are given life.

Bless the Church, that she may be fruitful in good works ... Let the word of truth not wither away, but grow to a rich harvest.

Come to the stony places of the world, where the life of the flesh prevails over the life of the spirit, and bring your peace.

May our families and friends, our neighbours and colleagues, receive the grace of the Spirit, to be rich in good work and sure faith.

Have mercy on those who are oppressed by care and have lost the way that they once knew . . . Bring them back into the way of love.

Through the Spirit that raised Jesus from the dead, give life to those who have died to this world.

May our prayers be as the good seed bearing fruit for the Kingdom of God.

PROPER 11

Let us pray to God, giver of all good gifts and our only defence against evil.

As we look for the full revelation of your glory, keep us faithful in work and worship . . . Defend the Church against the assaults of evil, to yield a good harvest from the planting of your holy word.

Root out all the evil things that mar the goodness of your world . . . Give the glorious liberty of the Spirit to those who live only for the demands of the flesh.

Shield our families from all assaults of evil . . . Bless our local community and keep it free from corruption . . . Guide with your Holy Spirit those who hold responsibility for health and environment.

Visit the afflicted with the assurance that their suffering will pass . . . Restore health to the damaged bodies and the troubled minds.

Grant that the faithful departed may as joint heirs with
Christ share in his glory ... Have mercy on all souls
in the time of judgement when good and evil shall be
revealed together.

May these our prayers, purified from fault and error,
be heard through Jesus Christ, Son of Man and Lord
of all.

PROPER 12

Let us pray to God, by whose grace we are members
of the Kingdom of Heaven.

Called to your service, may we and the whole Church
be faithful in all things ... Grant that we shall be good
stewards of the great treasure entrusted to us.

Reveal the true treasure of your word to those
whose eyes are closed by the cares of this world ...
Plant the seed that shall grow up into a better life for
all.

Make us conquerors through Christ of all that would
harm our living together with others ... May our
whole community grow towards your Kingdom.

Give to those who suffer the assurance that they are
not forgotten, never separated from the love of Christ
... May his sufferings for humanity relieve their
troubles.

When the time of judgement is fulfilled, look with
mercy on the souls of the departed ... By the merits
of Christ, let them not be lost in that day.

Trusting in the mercy of God, the Judge of all, we
submit our prayers in the name of Christ.

PROPER 13

Let us pray to God, the bountiful Giver, for the needs of the Church and of all people ...

We give thanks for the grace that always exceeds what we can hope or ask ... As we are fed by word and sacrament, make us strong in your service.

Feed the spiritual hunger of the world where many are lost in desert places, far from their true home ... Come to those who know you only partially and bring them into the perfect light.

Show us the way to relieve the needs that lie close to us ... Take our small offerings and make them great in your service.

May the compassion of Christ still prevail to heal the sick and feed the hungry, through the divine love that never fails.

Grant refreshment, light and peace to those who no longer need the bread of this world ... Receive them into their eternal home.

Strengthened by our spiritual food, we pray with confidence in the generous love of Christ.

PROPER 14

Let us pray to God, who rules all things in heaven and on earth.

Fill the Church with the zeal of the Gospel, that your word may go out into all the world ... With eyes fixed upon our Saviour, may your people never fail in faith.

Calm the storms that trouble the world ... Through the word of truth, bring a new vision of Christ who is close to all but unseen by many.

Grant that we shall live in peace with all around us ... Give to our community the spirit of mutual love, that all may be one in you ... May Christ, always present among us, draw us all to himself.

Bear up those who sink beneath the waves of pain and sorrow ... Bring them close to you in perfect trust.

Receive into your care the dead who have heard and trusted in your word ... Have mercy on those whose faith was weak but in their lives sought to reach you.

That the power of Christ may uphold us in peril and in our weakness, we pray in his name.

PROPER 15

To God who loves the world that he has made, let us pray for ourselves and for all people.

As you have given to your people the gift of faith, make that faith powerful as a witness to your love ... Let your Church be constant in prayer, never doubting your power to save.

Gather into your fold the lost sheep of this world, the unbelievers, the hard of heart ... Hear those who desire to know you but cannot speak their need.

Guide and guard our families and all others with whom we share our lives ... Bless the homes where there is sickness or any other trouble.

Bring healing to children who are ill or in pain ... Comfort and strengthen parents who are anxious for their children ... Give peace to all unquiet minds and troubled spirits.

Give peace to the dead who had no peace in their dying ... Have compassion on those who died without faith, that they too may receive your mercy.

Fed at the Table of the Lord, we ask him to accept our faith and pardon our unworthiness.

PROPER 16

Let us pray for the Church which Christ has built and for the world which he has saved.

Preserve your Church in strength and stability, by your promise that no evil shall prevail against it ... Make its members zealous in their callings, to work in all things according to your will.

Give to all people the desire to work together for good ... As they recognise their calling, may each come to know Christ as the Son of God.

Bless us in our daily work and bless those who work with us ... Use in your service the abilities of all who live and work in this community ... Grant wisdom and discernment to those who are called to special responsibility.

Strengthen with hope those who think themselves of no worth ... Give them light to understand their part in your purpose and grace to fulfil it.

We commend those who have died in the faith of Christ, true to the Church which he built ... Keep us constant in the same faith now and at the last.

Confessing Christ as the Son of God, we pray in his name.

PROPER 17

Let us pray for the Church of Christ, and for his reign over all the world.

Confirm your faithful people in the peace and harmony that is your will for them ... May the Church never fail to proclaim the Cross of Christ, the salvation of the world.

Give to all people hope in place of despair, patience in place of unrest, love in place of anger ... Enlighten with the truth of the Gospel those whose desire is only for the things of this world.

Give us true peace in our homes and in our work ... Reconcile with your healing power all disputes and hostility among us ... Let no selfish desires damage our relationships with others.

Have mercy on those who feel they are overcome by evil and have lost their way ... Bring them to see that in their affliction they are following the steps of Jesus.

Receive into your gracious care those who have followed the way of the Cross to the end ... Save, even at the last, souls in peril from corruption by this world.

Trusting in the Cross of Christ our Saviour, we pray in his name.

PROPER 18

Let us pray in love to God who loves all that he has made.

Let the whole Church be filled with the divine grace which comes where two or three are gathered together in your name ... Bless your Christian people with unity to empower their prayers.

Rouse the world from the sloth of selfish and material concerns ... Heal with the spirit of love the disputes that divide people and nations.

Bless our families, friends and neighbours with the spirit of reconciliation ... Let your law be fulfilled among us in words of love.

Come and relieve those who are caught in bitter litigation ... Help the victims of injustice who suffer under loveless power.

We pray for those who have tried to follow the way of love and are now at rest ... In the fullness of your love, give them perfect freedom.

Gathered together in the name of Christ, we make our prayers through him.

PROPER 19

Let us pray to God, trusting in his mercy to all who call upon him in faith.

Guard the Church from too much concern for lesser things ... Grant us grace to keep reverence and order but to seek first the salvation of souls.

May those who work in the world of finance be just and compassionate in their dealings ... Give them wisdom, and the grace to use their skill not as an end but for the welfare of all.

Give us tolerance as we live and work with others ... Since none can live to themselves alone, help us to care for our community.

Have mercy on all distressed by debt or financial worry ... Turn by your grace the hearts of those who oppress the poor and needy.

Have mercy, even at the last, on the greedy and unforgiving ... Help us so to forgive that in the hour of death we may be forgiven.

In the spirit of forgiving, as we trust to be forgiven, we offer these our prayers.

PROPER 20

Let us pray to God, who has called us to serve him in our work and in our worship.

Give to your faithful people grace to live for the good of this world, knowing that our true life is yet to come . . . Make our lives worthy of the name of Christ which we confess.

Bring justice and harmony into the workplaces of the world . . . Make selfishness give way to desire for the common good.

Teach us to be generous in our work, considerate to those who work with us . . . Bless in your service the daily work of our community.

Have mercy on the unemployed and grant them the dignity of work that they desire . . . Have mercy also on those whose work is long and heavy . . . Sustain them in the heat and burden of the day.

May your perpetual light shine on those who have gone into the better life . . . Keep us always ready to depart and be closer to Christ who is already with us here.

Seeking no reward but the faithful service of God, we offer our prayers to him.

PROPER 21

By the authority of Christ, given to his Church, let us pray to the Lord.

Give to the Church the spirit of service and humility by the power of Jesus Christ who became man for our sake . . . Keep your people obedient in all things, even to the death of the body.

Dispel the pride that holds people apart from people and nation from nation . . . Make your power acknowledged and your will accomplished through all the world.

Visit and heal with your love those whose lives come close to ours but are divided by pride and self-will . . . May the mind of Jesus direct us in all our relationships.

Help those whose suffering is the result of their own selfishness . . . Bring them out of their darkness into the freedom of obedience to your service.

We remember those who have followed Jesus until death . . . As he is highly exalted, raise them with him into your eternal presence.

Strengthened in our weakness by the divine humility of Christ, we make our prayers in his name.

PROPER 22

In the power of the Son, let us pray to God who governs all in heaven and earth.

Inspire your Church always to press forward to the goal to which she is called . . . Make all her members faithful servants of your will.

Look with mercy on a world when the greed of gain deprives many of their rights . . . Guide those in authority to govern by the true values of your Kingdom.

In all our dealings with others, teach us not to trust our own desires but to follow where Christ has led

. . . Make us honest in our work, seeking the good of others.

Have mercy on those who have been made poor by the dishonesty of others . . . Relieve their needs and give them the hope of renewal in your purpose for them.

We give thanks for those who have come by the power of Christ to the resurrection of the dead . . . Grant that we shall not lose through sin our inheritance in your eternal Kingdom.

We offer our prayers, entreating that we may be faithful inheritors of the Kingdom.

PROPER 23

Let us pray to the Father who invites all men and women to receive his love.

Grant that your people, called by grace, shall be worthy of their calling . . . Keep the Church faithful in proclaiming all the good things of your giving.

Let the whole world hear your call . . . Come to those who turn away and gather them into the great feast of your love.

Reconcile those in our community who are at variance with each other . . . Draw us, our families and friends, into the peace that is beyond our understanding.

Be with your servants who suffer for their proclaiming of the Gospel . . . Turn the hearts of their persecutors and bring them to the way of truth.

Grant your peace to the faithful departed, that they may enjoy the perfection of those good things which they partially knew in this world.

We pray as those who seek to be worthy guests of the Lord who has called us to his divine feast.

PROPER 24

Let us pray to God, who is rightfully to be honoured by all that he has made.

As you have given grace to your Church through the Holy Spirit, grant that her members may show that grace by word and deed in their lives.

May all who are concerned in the affairs of this world remember the honour due to you ... Enlighten all in authority with the spirit of justice and mercy.

Help us so to live that we shall be good examples to our neighbours and colleagues ... Guide in honesty and fair dealing those who do business in this community.

Heal the minds that are warped by bitterness and the wish to harm others ... Have mercy on all who are deprived of their true joy by love of vain things.

May the power of the risen Christ, who saves us from the wrath to come, grant to the departed refreshment, light and peace.

We pray that our lives may be obedient and our offerings sincere in the faith of Christ.

PROPER 25

Let us pray to the Lord who rules over all things on earth and in heaven.

May your Church always proclaim the Gospel entrusted to her, never to be turned aside by desire for popular approval or worldly glory ... May she fulfil in all her works the great commandment of your love.

Draw the nations closer to the sharing of love that overcomes all differences ... Hasten the time when the whole world shall acknowledge you as Lord of all.

In love and gentleness may we be ministers of your grace to all those with whom we share our lives ... Help us to live together as true neighbours of one another.

Have mercy on all who have been led astray and harmed by false teaching ... Forgive their errors and free them from the power of evil.

Raise up the faithful departed into the perfect love which they began to understand in this world ... Have mercy on those who did not understand, and grant them now the joy and fellowship that they could not find here.

We make our prayers in holy love to God and to our neighbours.

or **BIBLE SUNDAY**

Let us pray to God, by whose word we are taught to pray.

Keep the Church faithful to the truth revealed in holy scripture ... Enrich your people with the word of Christ, for unity of purpose and for witness to the world.

Make the glory of your word shine throughout the world, to be a light to all people ... Bless those who work to make your word known among the nations ... Be their support in times of trouble and their defence against hostility.

Guide and enable us to spread the good news of salvation among our families and friends, our colleagues and neighbours ... Give to all in this community the love of your word, and bless those who are seeking you through study of the Bible.

Look with compassion on all who are deprived of Bible reading, through ignorance, poverty or lack of translation in their own tongues ... Create and satisfy in them true desire for your living word.

We pray for those who strove to live by the teachings of scripture and whose longing for your word is now perfectly fulfilled ... Grant that we too may be kept securely in the way of salvation.

Guided by the word of God made known to us, we pray in faith.

DEDICATION FESTIVAL

Let us pray to God, who has given the Church to be a light to the world.

Bless this church, that it may be the temple of the living God, an assembly of those on whom your favour rests ... Keep it free from all that would profane its worship or demean its witness.

Wherever a building is dedicated to your service, make it a beacon of truth and hope to all around ... Cleanse and heal all the places where religion is tainted by love of worldly gain.

May our church be known throughout this community as a place where all may come in hope and joy ... Give us courtesy to welcome, and sensitivity to discern the needs of visitors.

Visit with your love those who are held back from coming to church through guilt and fear, through scorn and pride or through indifference . . . Draw them into the Christian fellowship which is the assembly of the faithful.

We give thanks for all who have worshipped in this church in past years . . . Though we see them no more, grant us continuing union through prayer until the day when we join with them in the perfect worship of heaven.

In this house of God, we humbly offer him our prayers.

ALL SAINTS' SUNDAY

Let us pray to God, whose saints have witnessed to his glory.

May your Church, built on the foundation of the saints, be faithful to the teaching of Jesus so that in all her life she may reveal his likeness . . . Let our prayers be united with the praise of the blessed in heaven.

We pray for the world that is so often deaf to the only teaching that can bring true joy . . . Grant to this generation the spirit that inspired the saints, that all may walk in way of righteousness.

Teach us to recognise the holiness of other people . . . Give to us, our families and friends, grace to live as Jesus taught his disciples.

Have mercy on those who are in great tribulation, persecuted for the sake of the Gospel . . . Bring relief in their distress, and the assurance of your blessing for all who are steadfast in faith.

Grant to the faithful departed a share in the inheritance of the saints . . . As we offer our prayers for them, may their heavenly prayers avail for us as we continue on our early pilgrimage . . . Bring us at last to the same blessedness.

Rejoicing in the fellowship of the saints, we pray that our prayers may be sanctified.

or FOURTH SUNDAY BEFORE ADVENT

Let us pray to God, the ruler of all, the beginning and the end.

Keep your Church free from temptation to conceal or darken the truth that she should proclaim . . . Shield us from error and false doctrine and from compromise with ways that are not yours.

Come with power to a world where many are led astray as they seek in other ways the assurance that you alone can give . . . Bring order to the confusion of their lives, and hope in their fears.

Give us gentle spirits, to help and comfort those with whom we live . . . Keep us, our families, friends and neighbours, in continual trust, not fearing what the future may bring.

Have compassion on refugees and all who have been forced to flee from their homes . . . Protect especially the mothers and the little children . . . In your mercy shorten the time of their distress.

Receive and pardon the souls of those who in this world followed the wrong paths and lived in error . . . Save them through the mercy of Christ who loved them although they did not know him.

We pray in the name of Christ, the true Messiah.

THIRD SUNDAY BEFORE ADVENT

In the spirit of divine wisdom, let us pray to the Lord.

Keep us ever watchful, alert to the signs of your presence both now and in time to come ... Give wisdom to all who serve your Church, making them always open to your call and ready in obedience.

Come with power wherever there is lack of purpose, where the world is marred by sloth and indifference ... Lead the nations out of darkness into the glorious light of your Kingdom.

Bless our families, our friends and neighbours, with wisdom that is careful without anxiety, provident without meanness ... Teach us to make good use of all your gifts to us.

Have mercy on those who are brought low by their own folly ... Hear their cry, even in the midnight of their distress, and give them new purpose ... Give assurance of new and greater life to all who fear death.

We give thanks for those who sleep in Jesus ... Keep us always ready to be called with them ... Comfort those who mourn, giving hope in their sorrow.

That we may hear the voice of Christ, the heavenly Bridegroom, we pray in his name.

SECOND SUNDAY BEFORE ADVENT

Let us pray to God, the only giver of power for good.

May all who confess your name be faithful stewards of what has been entrusted to them ... As we look for the coming of Christ, we pray that the Church on earth may always be ready to become one with the Church of the blessed in heaven.

Where business is done in the world, drive out dishonesty and self-seeking ... Bring to all people the knowledge that this world is not the end ... As we work for the present good, let our eyes be lifted to the future glory.

Draw into your service all in our community that they may be used for the coming of the Kingdom ... Shine your love on us, our families and friends, that we may live as children of the light.

Have mercy on those who have not fulfilled the best that is in them, hindered by sloth or circumstance or self-doubt ... Rouse them to be active in doing your will.

We pray for those who have come to their last day and passed into new life ... Confident that waking or sleeping we are with Christ, we pray that we shall be always ready to hear his call.

That we may faithfully respond to the grace given to us, we offer our prayers.

CHRIST THE KING

Let us pray to God, King of heaven and Lord of all the world.

Bless the Church, the Body of Christ, and make her worthy to claim him as her head ... Guide your ministers to be good shepherds of their flocks, faithful in word and works.

Spread through the world the spirit of love and care ... Bless those who work to relieve suffering ... May all the nations acknowledge Christ as King of kings and Lord of lords.

Inspire our community with concern for those in need
... Help us to spread to our neighbours and those
with whom we work the good news of Christ as Lord.

Have mercy on all who are in want of food or drink
or clothing, the sick and those in prison ... Through
human hands, bring them the relief that comes from
your love and power.

We pray for those who have been called from this
world to be with Christ ... By his kingship of the
living and the dead, grant them rest.

We pray with confidence in the name of Christ the
King.

Principal Service

Year B

FIRST SUNDAY OF ADVENT

Let us pray as faithful servants to know and obey the will of God.

Make your Church ever watchful to discern the signs of your will . . . Keep her firm and constant to the end, knowing that all her works are worth nothing without the blessing of your grace.

Come with great power to a world where many are ignorant of your purposes . . . Give to those in authority wisdom to know you and to lead others in the right way.

Give to us, our families and friends, discernment to recognise your presence among us at all times . . . May we grow in the grace that Christ gives to all who will come to him.

Have mercy on those who trust in their own works and do not know their need . . . Give the vision of your glory to those whose eyes are darkened by affliction.

We pray for those who have heard your call and met the hour of their death . . . Have mercy on them, with the grace that alone gives salvation.

We pray in the name of Christ who has come among us and is to come again.

SECOND SUNDAY OF ADVENT

Let us pray that the good news of salvation may inspire the Church and all the world.

As you have given the message of hope and comfort to your people in all ages, fill the Church with zeal to proclaim the Gospel of Christ ... Make your people, sealed by baptism and the Holy Spirit, to be one in your Kingdom.

Make straight the crooked places of the world and lead the nations into the way of peace ... Reveal your glory so that all people shall see it and become your own.

Bless us, our families and friends, that we may seek the good and avoid the evil ... Save us from the judgement of having neglected your word.

Be close to those who do your work in obscurity and poverty ... Give them the comfort of your presence and shield them from danger and persecution.

We pray for those who have come out of the wilderness into new life ... Look upon them with the eyes of mercy, counting them righteous not for their merit but through the love of Christ.

We join our voices with all those which speak of the Gospel of Christ.

THIRD SUNDAY OF ADVENT

Let us pray to God, the source of all light and life.

Send your spirit upon the Church, for the declaration of the Gospel to all nations ... Give to your people the prophetic voice that brings knowledge of salvation through Jesus Christ.

Restore to new life the places that human sin and folly have made desolate ... Guide into the true light of repentance those who work wrath and destruction ... Lead all nations to be one in the name of Christ.

Make us your messengers among our friends and neighbours, and all with whom we share our lives ... Bless to a rich harvest all the signs of hope and growth in our community.

Bring freedom to those who are unjustly in captivity and those who are imprisoned in their own despair ... Comfort and raise up to new life those whose hearts are broken by sorrow.

We give thanks for all who have heard the message of salvation and passed from this world into the full knowledge of Christ ... Keep us constant in faith until we too shall come to him.

We pray, confident in the grace of baptism and led by the light of Christ.

FOURTH SUNDAY OF ADVENT

Let us pray to the Lord who has brought salvation to all who will hear his word.

Bless all the places where your people meet for worship, but keep us from valuing them more highly than the knowledge that you are present everywhere ... Grant us the faith and trust that was in Mary, to be always ready to receive your word.

By the Holy Spirit who came to Mary, bring peace and good will among all the nations ... Lead the rulers of this world to acknowledge your lordship and to exercise their power in the obedience of faith.

Give to us, our families and friends, ears eager to hear you and eyes open to perceive you . . . Be with women in our community who are expecting new babies and bring them to safe and joyful birth.

Have mercy on the homeless, the refugees and the wanderers of this world and grant them secure shelter . . . Be close to women who bear their children in strange and unwelcoming places.

We pray for those who have died, having had no settled home in this world . . . Give them rest in the heavenly home where in your mercy there is space for all.

Rejoicing in the good news brought to the blessed Virgin Mary, we offer our prayers.

CHRISTMAS DAY

As for Year A, p. 4.

FIRST SUNDAY OF CHRISTMAS

Let us pray to the Father who has revealed his glory by the Incarnation of the Son.

Now and at all times inspire the Church to proclaim the good news of the Son of God, through whom his people have become God's children . . . Make us fervent with the new law of love that we have received from him.

Grant to the simple and humble people of this world the vision of the shepherds who rejoiced at the birth of Jesus . . . May the divine glory and goodness shine upon all nations.

Give grace to our families, that we may meditate with Mary upon the mystery of the Incarnation . . . Inspire with the true joy of Christmas those among whom we work and grant them peace in their daily lives.

Have mercy on all whose lives are constrained by falsehood and superstition . . . Let your Spirit come into their hearts to set them free, sharing in the glory of human nature renewed.

We pray for those who have often celebrated this holy time and have passed through a new birth into eternal life . . . As they were once adopted into your family on earth, we rejoice with them that they are for ever with you, their heavenly Father.

Rejoicing with those who first saw the incarnate Christ, we pray in his name.

SECOND SUNDAY OF CHRISTMAS

Because the Word was made flesh for our salvation, we are confident to pray.

Called to your service not by our merits but by your grace, we pray for firmness in the faith that has been revealed to us . . . As we have received grace, so make our lives truly gracious in worship of you and in service of others.

Gather all things together in Christ, that this world may be as one with the Kingdom of Heaven . . . May the light of Christ shine on all who do not know him, that they may be born again in faith.

In all our human relationships, let us remember that we are children of one divine Father . . . Bless all in our local community with the knowledge of their calling and the grace to fulfil it.

Have mercy on all whose lives lack purpose and direction . . . Reveal your will to them, illuminate them with your light to see that they too are your children.

We give thanks for those who have trusted in the Word made flesh and shown his grace in their lives, and whose hope is now fulfilled . . . Keep us in the same hope, that we in time may share their joy.

Thankful for the grace and truth revealed in Christ, we pray through him.

THE EPIPHANY

As for Year A, p. 7.

THE BAPTISM OF CHRIST (FIRST SUNDAY OF EPIPHANY)

Let us pray to the Father who glorified his beloved Son in his baptism as a sign to the world.

Grant to all who are made members of your Church by baptism the grace of the Holy Spirit to live worthily of their calling . . . Give to your people both repentance for their sins and strength in the good works prepared for them to do.

Come into the hearts of all who do not know you, and those who know you only imperfectly . . . Let the people of this world no longer walk in darkness, but in the light of truth.

We pray for all who at this time are preparing for baptism . . . Fill them with your grace, so that in due time they may show that grace in their lives . . .

Strengthen parents and godparents to be faithful in their promises.

Pardon and turn to repentance those who have chosen to live in the darkness of sin ... Come to those who have followed dangerous and forbidden ways and lead them into new life.

Grant rest and peace to the faithful who, having once died to sin in the water of baptism, have now died to this world ... Lighten them with the light that has been your gift to all creation from the beginning.

United in baptism, we join our prayers with those of all the people of God.

SECOND SUNDAY OF EPIPHANY

Let us pray to the Father who through the Son has opened the way to heaven.

May your Church be always alert in your service, ready to answer new calls for the coming of the Kingdom ... Lift up our hearts to adore the Lamb who was slain for our salvation.

Cast out the distrust that separates people of different cultures and backgrounds ... Draw all to be of one mind, open to the heavenly message that Christ has brought into the world.

Be present among our families, our friends, our colleagues ... If any are called to particular service in your purpose, give them ears to hear and wills to follow you.

Have mercy on the aged whose powers are failing and whose eyes grow dim; give them your strength to replace their own ... Support little children who are perplexed by responsibilities beyond their years.

We give thanks for all who have grown old in your service and have passed to rest ... Give us grace to follow their example and to be vigilant to the end.

As followers of Christ, called to his service, we pray in his name.

THIRD SUNDAY OF EPIPHANY

Let us pray to God, whose love to all that he has made is beyond measure.

Make your Church always worthy of her calling as the Bride of Christ ... Give to all Christian people the virtues of faith and purity that shall show your glory before the world.

Bless the love which brings men and women together into a new unity ... Be near to those soon to be married or recently married, and give them grace to continue in love and loyalty to the end of their lives.

Come with your generous care into our homes and into all the homes of this community ... Bless the mothers who are careful for so many needs, and refresh them when they are weary.

Look with mercy on those homes where love is threatened by poverty ... Support and strengthen the parents who struggle to provide for their children.

We rejoice with those who take their part in the great supper of Christ, the Lamb of God ... May the good wine of our communion here be a seal of our eternal life hereafter.

Called to the feast of our Lord, we pray to be worthy of our calling.

FOURTH SUNDAY OF EPIPHANY

Let us pray to God, our only defence and refuge against evil.

Grant to the Church the voice of prophecy, to proclaim your word and lead the world into the way of truth ... Give power to those who preach, that they may be confident in the name of Christ by whose authority they speak.

Let your call come to the rulers of nations and leaders of peoples throughout the world, so that they may know that true power is from you alone ... Bless those who work to make your word known in all lands.

Grant that we may have wisdom and opportunity to speak of our faith to others ... Make us instruments of your peace to our families and friends, our neighbours and those with whom we work ... Give new light to those who do not know you.

Have mercy on those who are in the power of evil ... Heal and restore all whose minds have been disturbed through occult practices ... Draw back into the way of truth those who are slipping into dangerous paths.

We pray for any who have died tormented in mind and spirit ... Grant them in death the peace and purity that they lost in this world and make them wholly yours for ever.

That we may be cleansed from our sins and freed from all harm, we pray through Christ our Lord.

THE PRESENTATION OF CHRIST

As for Year A, p. 11.

ORDINARY TIME

PROPER 1

Let us pray to God for the healing of all that mars the perfection of his creation.

Guide the Church to preach your word with power and confidence, but with sensitivity to the needs of each individual . . . Give your people wisdom to know when to be firm and when to give way . . . Be with us both in public worship and in silent recollection of your presence.

Let all people look on the wonders of your creation and praise your power . . . In towns and cities and in the lonely places bring your healing presence to heal the fever of our world.

Teach us to be servants of all, helpful to those with whom we pass our lives . . . Come into our homes to calm our unrest and ease our troubles.

We pray for the sick, especially those known to us, who are in our hearts at this time . . . Comfort and relieve those who suffer in mind or body . . . Give skill and compassion to all who do the work of healing.

We give thanks for those who, drawing their strength from you in this world, have yielded their souls into your care . . . Pardon whatever sins they have committed, that they may be clean before you in the new life.

That we may be whole in body, mind and spirit, we pray through Christ the healer.

PROPER 2

Let us pray to God, who rejects none who come to him in faith.

Grant that we who confess the faith of Christ may run the race that is set before us, looking for no reward but that of doing your will ... Give us discernment to see you in the little things as well as in the great, and to obey whatever you may command.

Break the pride of human power that will not accept the simplicity of divine truth ... Show the way to those who walk through the world without direction or purpose.

In your compassion, give wholeness and strength to us, to our families and friends and neighbours ... Teach us to live with joy in the pleasures which you grant us but never to let them come between ourselves and our calling in you.

Have mercy on all who suffer from diseases that bring scorn and rejection as well as bodily suffering ... Bless and guide those who seek cures for what has seemed incurable ... Give patience and love to those who care for the chronically ill.

We pray for those who died as outcasts because their sickness was judged harshly by those around them ... Make them whole in your presence, restored by the love that they could not find in this world.

We pray that our unworthiness may be made worthy by the healing power of Christ.

PROPER 3

Let us pray to God, who forgives our sins and heals our infirmities.

Giving praise for all your mercies towards us, we pray that the Church may ever be mindful of the benefits received ... Grant to your ministers grace to preach the

Gospel without doubt or reservation, making known the good news of your patient and pardoning love.

Look with mercy on a world where love is often met with cynicism and suspicion . . . Grant that the nations shall not be held in the old ways of hostility but brought into a new freedom where each may work together for the good of all.

Make us agents of your care in our community, to comfort and aid the sick and disabled . . . Let compassion be the sign of our faith, drawing all those among whom we live closer to each other and to you.

Have mercy on those who are held back by crippling disease from the fullness of life . . . Be with them, and those who care for them . . . Enrich with mutual love all the many relationships of dependence.

We give thanks for those you have made for yourself and who now rejoice in the fullness of new life . . . We remember those who suffered infirmity in the body and are made whole at last.

Laying our prayers at the feet of Christ, we offer them in his name.

SECOND SUNDAY BEFORE LENT

Let us pray to the Father who sent the Son to be the Light of the world.

Give wisdom to the Church, to see the way of her mission and to give good counsel to all who seek . . . As she proclaims the Word made flesh, let his light shine through her ministry to the whole world.

Give true light to the world where many walk in darkness believing that their own efforts make them wise

... Let all know that they may be your children through faith and find your peace.

Inspire and direct all in our community who teach and guide others ... Fill them with wisdom and understanding and use them in your service to reconcile those who are estranged and to make the dark places bright.

Restore those who are tormented by guilt and have not sought mercy through the Cross ... Lighten their darkness, calm their fears and make their lives whole again.

We rejoice with those who have passed through darkness into a greater light ... Confirm and strengthen our own trust in the Word made flesh, that we may at last share in their joy.

May our words be offered in the name of Christ, the eternal Word.

SUNDAY BEFORE LENT

Let us pray to God, whose glory is revealed through the Church to all the world.

May your wonderful light transfigure the Church, changing human weakness into divine strength ... Keep us faithful in this generation to the mission of preaching and prophecy which we have received from those who went before us in the faith and have left us their example.

Let not the Gospel be hidden beneath the cares and struggles of the world ... In concern for the present time, grant that the wisdom of the past shall not be forgotten as a guide to people and nations.

As we seek to follow you, enable us also to lead others towards you ... Shine with the light of your truth upon us, our families and friends and neighbours.

Have mercy on all who have suffered the loss of one whom they loved and trusted ... Comfort them with the assurance of new life to come ... Strengthen them to continue their lives in this world according to your will for them.

We pray for all who gone from this world into your nearer presence ... In the light of heaven, may they join the praise given by your worshippers through all the ages.

We pray in the name of Christ, revealed in glory to his disciples throughout all ages.

ASH WEDNESDAY

As Year A, p. 16.

FIRST SUNDAY OF LENT

For deliverance from temptation and grace in our Lenten resolutions, let us pray to the Lord.

As we are sealed your own by baptism, grant to us the spirit of repentance for sin and resolution for good ... Strengthen the Church to be a refuge from evil, open to all who will come in faith.

We pray for the created world, sustained by your mercy but threatened by human greed and indifference ... Teach us to live in better harmony with the seasons of the year and with all our fellow-creatures.

Enable the teachers and youth leaders in this community to lead the young into the right way ... Give grace to parents and godparents to fulfil their promises for the children they bring to baptism.

Have mercy on victims of floods and other natural disasters ... Bring relief in areas where nature is harsh and living difficult ... Give strength to those who work to reclaim the waste places of the world.

We give thanks for those who have found peace through the saving death of Christ ... We pray that we like them may share in the power of his Resurrection.

We pray through Jesus Christ, tempted, as we are, yet without sin.

SECOND SUNDAY OF LENT

Let us pray to God, who calls us to follow him and to confess his holy name.

We pray for the Church, in which we are heirs of Abraham and his promised race, restored in Christ ... We pray for faithfulness in following where Christ has led, not counting the cost of the discipleship to which we are called.

May the nations of the world recognise their common humanity, and cease from the hostility that causes separation ... Give freedom from the consuming desire for material gain ... Restore the joy of your salvation to all who have been drawn away from their spiritual path.

As we pray for our families, we remember all the parents of children and young people ... Help them in their responsibility, that they may provide for their families both in material and spiritual needs.

Visit and comfort those who cannot have the children that they desire ... Draw the old and lonely into the love of the wider family that confesses your name.

We pray for the departed of all the ages, who have heard your promise and followed your calling ... As we are their descendants on earth, grant that we may share with them the life of heaven.

We ask that our prayers may be worthy of our calling as disciples of Christ.

THIRD SUNDAY OF LENT

In holiness and reverence, let us pray to the Lord of the Church and of all creation.

Keep your Church secure from the dangers of worldliness and greed ... Give grace to your ministers, to preach the Gospel of Christ and to fulfil your commandments both in their words and in their lives.

Pity the world where ignorance and prejudice often rule ... Give true wisdom to all in authority ... Pardon and cleanse the individuals and organisations whose goodness has been corrupted by love of gain.

Bless our families and keep them in purity of faith and righteousness of living ... Strengthen those in our community who have responsibility for teaching and training, that they may give leadership in the way you have commanded.

Have mercy on those who suffer because they have fallen into evil ways ... Restore them to the freedom that is found in Christ alone ... Comfort and relieve the victims of lust, dishonesty and violence.

We pray for those who have died in the body, that they may be raised in Christ ... Bring them to the joy of your heavenly Temple, where worship is perfect and eternal.

We pray that we may be worthy to worship in the Temple of the Lord.

FOURTH SUNDAY OF LENT

Let us pray to God, that in his light we may see light.

Forgive your people for the discontent and self-will that hinders your loving purpose . . . Grant that, trusting in Christ alone, the Church may fulfil all that you have ordained.

Let your light so shine in the world that all eyes shall be lifted to see the salvation of the Cross . . . Have pity on nations locked in conflict and give them the peace that Christ has brought.

Give grace to us, to our families and friends, that we may see clearly the way in which we should walk . . . Increase our faith and make us a light to others.

Have mercy on those who are driven to despair by hunger and poverty . . . Forgive them when they deny you in their misery, and grant them healing in body and soul.

As we remember the departed, we pray that they may be pardoned for the sins of this life and receive salvation in Christ . . . Raise them up into the fullness of your presence.

We pray in the name of the Son of God who was given that we might have eternal life.

or **MOTHERING SUNDAY** see p. 158.

FIFTH SUNDAY OF LENT

Let us pray to the Lord whose glory has been revealed throughout all ages.

Grant to your faithful people grace so to die to this world that they may obey you in all things to the end . . . Make your priests and ministers faithful followers of Jesus Christ, our great High Priest, and servants of his new covenant.

As so many in the world seek for truth and cannot find the way, in your mercy reveal to them the hope that is in Christ ... Write your laws in the hearts of all people, that they may fully know you and find forgiveness for their sins.

Grant to us and to all whom we love the spirit of obedience to the command of Christ ... Help us to teach our neighbours and friends truly to know the Lord.

Have mercy on all who suffer, that they may know the sufferings of Christ and find comfort in him ... Give light to those who value their worldly pleasures too highly, and lead them to find their true selves in you.

We pray for those who have died, that you will grant them your salvation ... Draw them to yourself, to be lifted up into eternal life.

We lift our voices in prayer through Christ who was lifted up for our salvation.

PALM SUNDAY

As Year A, p. 21.

MAUNDY THURSDAY

As Year A, p. 22.

GOOD FRIDAY

As Year A, p. 23.

EASTER EVE

As Year A, p. 24.

EASTER DAY

As Year A, p. 24.

SECOND SUNDAY OF EASTER

Let us pray in faith to the Father who raised his Son from the dead.

Increase the faith of the Church, dispersing doubts and fears that hold us back from complete trust in you ... Heal divisions among Christians, making all of one heart and soul in faith to proclaim the power of the Resurrection.

Break through the closed doors of human hearts with the joy of the Risen Christ ... Make the desire for sharing and co-operation prevail over selfishness and greed ... Bring peace to the troubled places of the world.

May the spirit of love dwell among our families, friends and neighbours ... Admitting where we have offended, let us live in harmony with all.

Have mercy on those whose faith is clouded by doubt and who walk in darkness ... Restore them to the full joy of your salvation and give them peace.

Raise up with the breath of your power those who have died to this world ... Grant them the full vision of the risen Christ in whom they have eternal life.

Confident in the power of Christ in whom we have eternal life, we pray in his name.

THIRD SUNDAY OF EASTER

For the Church and for all people, let us pray to God, present among us now and always.

Rejoicing in the saving death and wonderful Resurrection of Christ, we seek the spirit of true repentance for sins committed ... Open the minds of your ministers, and give them deeper understanding of the good news which they preach.

Look with compassion on a world where the innocent still suffer and authority is often unjust ... Give wisdom to those who rule over others, and lead them into the way of compassion and love.

Grant that we shall know the presence of Christ in our families and among our friends ... May he always be the unseen guest at our meals, so that we may welcome others in his name.

Have mercy on all who suffer from the ignorance and malice of power misused ... Strengthen all who are persecuted for their witness to the truth.

We give thanks for the departed who are lifted up with Christ to eternal life ... May they rejoice in his risen and ascended glory.

With awe and reverence but in confidence, we offer our prayers.

FOURTH SUNDAY OF EASTER

Let us pray to God, who sent his Son to be the great Shepherd of his sheep.

Grant that the Church of Christ, assured that there is no other name given under heaven for salvation, may show forth his love in word and deed ... Make your ministers faithful shepherds of those entrusted to their care.

Draw the peoples of the world into the fold of your love, that they may love one another and cease from strife ... Defend them from false teachers and all that would lead them astray.

Bless our homes with the spirit of your love so that we and our families may live in Christ and he in us ... May he always be the true door of our going out and our coming in.

Be merciful to those who have been betrayed by those they trusted ... Comfort and relieve deserted wives and husbands, and children abandoned by their parents.

May Jesus Christ who laid down his life for his sheep, receive the departed into the good pastures of heaven ... In his saving name, grant them eternal joy.

That we may be gathered into the fold of Christ, we pray in his name.

FIFTH SUNDAY OF EASTER

Let us pray to God, who alone gives to his people the power for good.

Grant that your Church, constant in faith and love, may bring forth good fruit ... Give unity to all her branches in the strength of Christ, the true vine ... Make her ministers wise in the teaching of holy scripture.

Enlighten all in the world who earnestly desire to find the truth, and lead them to those who can show them the way ... With your love, cast out the fear that destroys fullness of life.

Bless those known to us who are preparing for adult baptism or church membership ... Keep us ready to help by our words and examples others who are seeking you.

Have mercy on those who are without security of living and have lost their sense of purpose ... Bring them back to the one sure source of life in Christ.

We pray for the departed, that their love may be made perfect in your presence ... Have pity on those whose lives on earth seemed withered and fruitless, that they may find fullness of life at last.

We offer our prayers through Christ, the source of our life and strength.

SIXTH SUNDAY OF EASTER

Let us pray to God in the love that he has shown and commanded.

Grant that your faithful people, chosen by your grace and sealed in baptism, may always proclaim your greatness by their deeds of love ... Bless and guide those who are working for the spread of the Gospel throughout the world.

May the power of love overcome the anger and bitterness that divides people and nations ... Send your Holy Spirit to heal all divisions and to make known the love of the Father which is revealed in Jesus Christ.

Make us gracious and loving in our relationships, that we may show ourselves to be those whom Jesus calls his friends ... Keep our families faithful to follow his commandment of love.

Have mercy on those who cannot love because they have never known love ... Visit with new life the outcast and neglected of our society ... Give us compassion and understanding when the will to love grows cold.

We give thanks for those who were called to be followers and friends of Jesus Christ in this world ... Receive them into eternal life with that divine love which they partly knew through the gift of human love.

Rejoicing that Christ has called us to be his friends, we make our prayers through him.

ASCENSION DAY

As Year A, p. 29.

SEVENTH SUNDAY OF EASTER

That all our lives may be sanctified in the truth, let us pray to the Lord.

We pray that your Church may be committed to the needs of the world, but never conformed to the world ... We pray that those you have called to your service may be strong in the faith of Christ and given power to reveal his love.

Be with all who must make decisions that will affect other lives ... Give wisdom to those who appoint or elect to positions of authority, guiding them with your Holy Spirit to seek the common good.

Bless us, our families and friends and colleagues in the decisions, both small and great, which we must make in our daily lives ... Unite us in the love that makes us your own, and keep us from all evil.

Have mercy on any who have broken faith, betraying those who trusted them ... Restore them in your mercy to the life of love that they have forsaken ... Guide us where we can bring relief to any who have lost direction through the distress of misplaced trust.

Grant to the faithful departed the eternal life promised through Jesus Christ ... May his saving love avail for those who have passed through this world and into the world beyond.

Since our joy is made complete in Christ, we pray with confidence in his name.

PENTECOST

As Year A, p. 31.

ORDINARY TIME

TRINITY SUNDAY

As Year A, p. 32.

PROPER 4

Let us pray to God, whose love heals all that is hurt and mends all that is broken.

Strengthen your Church in all dangers and difficulties, to witness to the faith that comes not from human strength but only from your grace ... Teach your people to maintain due reverence but never to set the forms of religion above the call of love.

Guide those who make and administer laws, to be both just and merciful in their calling ... Bless with peace and harmony the places where laws are good and for the benefit of all . . . Give courage to those who work to reform laws that are harsh and oppressive.

May your light shine upon us in all that brings us closer to others . . . Let all that darkens the life of this community be cast out by the life that is in Jesus.

Have mercy on all who suffer under unjust regimes . . . Bless and strengthen those who are persecuted for their faith . . . Grant healing to those who are afflicted in the use of their limbs.

We pray for the departed who acknowledged the saving death of Jesus and now rejoice in his eternal life . . . Have mercy on all who have died through human injustice, and grant them rest.

Rejoicing in the glorious freedom given us in Christ, we pray through him.

PROPER 5

Let us pray in the power of the Holy Spirit, the source of healing and grace.

Give to your Church grace to be constant in all the duties laid upon her, while looking always to the greater calling beyond this world . . . Heal her divisions and make her one in love, so that no evil can enter.

Come to the rulers of this world and make them know themselves to be responsible only to you, the Ruler of all . . . Give to all who desire the good of humanity a shared will and a common purpose to work freely together.

Be close to us in our families, healing the doubts and conflicts that may trouble us . . . Teach us also to know that all are members of our family, because they are yours.

Have mercy on those who have lost their power to resist the attacks of evil ... Bless and enable those who work to relieve their suffering ... Empower and protect exorcists and healers of mind and spirit.

As Jesus was raised from the dead, so grant resurrection and new life to those who have died trusting in him ... Though their outward bodies have perished, clothe them in the new garments of salvation.

We pray through Christ, by whom we are healed and empowered to be his people.

PROPER 6

For the increase of his Kingdom, let us pray to the Lord.

Fill your Church with confidence in Christ as her Lord, to make him known by teaching and example ... Nourish the good seed of your word in us, that it may be fruitful in witness to the world.

As Christ died for all, may his love renew men and women as his new creation ... Open the eyes that are closed to your glory and the ears that will not hear the good news ... Let self-interest be changed to a true desire for the common good.

Guide us to discern the signs of your presence among us, in family life, in work, in all our dealings ... Trusting in your strength, may we bring to fruition all that is your will for us.

Bless and comfort those whose work is hard and who see no result for what they do ... Give them strength to persevere, in the knowledge that you are working in all things.

We pray for those who have left their earthly bodies and come home to you ... Judge them with mercy through the sacrifice of Christ.

That we may grow in the service of Christ, we pray in his name.

PROPER 7

Let us pray to God, the protector of all people and nations.

Keep the Church constant in faith and works, secure against the conflicting demands of our time ... Armed with your righteousness and trusting in you alone, make your people ready to meet the needs of all.

Give peace to all places in the world that are torn by the storms of war and violence ... Come into the hearts of the powerful, giving them a desire to be reconciled with their enemies and to live in harmony ... Where there is hatred, let there be love.

In our work, let us remember that we are workers together with Jesus ... Give us grace to be mediators in disputes and to calm the tensions in our daily lives with others.

Have mercy on those who have no peace in themselves and bring them the peace of your presence ... Watch over sailors and all who travel by sea, and preserve them from danger.

We give thanks for those who have crossed from life through death, and have come to rest in life eternal ... Grant them a safe harbour and the peace that cannot be broken.

Trusting in Christ, ever present to save us, we pray in his name.

PROPER 8

For the healing of all that has fallen away from good, let us pray to the Lord.

Bless your Church with the humility that was in Christ ... Following him in poverty of spirit and lowliness of heart, may your people have grace to share the riches that he brought to fallen humanity.

Move with your Spirit the wills of those who control the resources of the world, that there may be a more just distribution of the good things which you have created ... Bring relief to those who suffer want, and lack even the necessities of life.

Give us grace to share the burdens of our friends and neighbours ... Guide us to listen and respond to those who call to us for help.

Have compassion on all who suffer with long and wasting diseases ... Give skill to doctors and nurses and patience to all who care for invalids.

We pray for those who have died in childhood ... Raise them up to complete and perfect life ... Comfort all who mourn for their little ones.

We pray in the name of Christ, by whom we are raised to new life.

PROPER 9

Let us pray to God, by whose authority we are called to his service.

Keep the Church steadfast, confident in the strength that comes only from your grace ... Bless those who are chosen as your ministers and messengers, that they may preach the Gospel with assurance ... Sustain those whose burdens are heavy as they work to relieve the burdens of others.

Wherever your word is preached, grant that it shall be heard with understanding and received with faith ... Change the hearts of those who glory in their own strength and authority, and teach them to bear their power humbly.

Give us wisdom to discern the gifts that you have given to our friends and colleagues ... Teach us to learn from one another and to give support where it is needed.

Uphold those who wish to help others but are frustrated by opposition and indifference ... Give grace to all who suffer, that they may be open to accept relief.

We give thanks for the departed who in this world were granted a partial vision of your wonder and to whom it is now revealed in its fullness ... Give us grace so to live in Christ that we too may behold his glory.

Through our prayers in the name of Christ, may we overcome evil.

PROPER 10

Let us pray to God whose righteousness is made known by his mighty word and works.

Keep your Church, called to be your messenger on earth and the channel of your grace, in faithful service of the Gospel . . . Defend her in adversity and give to your priests and ministers courage to witness in word and deed.

Turn the hearts of those who misuse their power over others . . . Bring hope and freedom to the places where people live in fear of tyranny and injustice.

As we have been made members of your family by adoption, bless our human families with your continual presence . . . Guide us to follow the way that you have prepared for us in all our relationships with others.

Have mercy on all who suffer for the sake of truth . . . Comfort those who are unjustly imprisoned and those who have been brought by human judgement into the shadow of death.

We pray for all who have died violently and alone . . . Grant them the peace that was denied them at their end and bring them to the joy of your heavenly Kingdom.

May the courage and fidelity of John the Baptist be our example as we pray.

PROPER 11

Let us pray to God who has compassion on his people in all their needs.

Strengthen the Church to be the witness of your new law and a living sign of your reconciling power . . . Bless those who work for the spread of the Gospel, granting them rest and refreshment when they are weary.

Save with your healing power the nations of the world . . . Grant that men and women shall not live in suspicion of strangers and fear of what seems to be foreign, but in harmony as your gathered people.

Draw into the fellowship of your household our families and friends, our neighbours and colleagues ... Make us one in the unity that Christ has brought.

Visit and relieve the sick ... Give new hope to those whose suffering has been long ... Give skill and compassion to all who do the work of healing.

We give thanks for those whose lives were built on the foundation of Jesus Christ and now rest in him ... Give them joy in the fellowship of the heavenly Church where he reigns for ever.

As sheep who have found their shepherd, we pray through Christ our Lord.

PROPER 12

Let us pray to God who gives to his people both bodily and spiritual food.

Guide the Church to feed your flock as Christ wonderfully fed the multitude ... Make your faithful people, being rooted and grounded in love, instruments of your love to all people.

We pray for all in the world who do not know the name of Christ or will not honour him ... Give to the learned knowledge of the love that is beyond knowledge, and to the rich understanding of the true riches of your glory.

Since the whole family of heaven and earth is named by you, give grace to our families to reflect your perfect love in our human love ... Bless those in our community who work to bring food and comfort to the infirm and to those in want.

Have mercy on those who lack the food that they need
... Prosper all efforts to relieve hunger in the world
... Grant help and courage to all who cannot properly
feed those they love.

We pray for all who have died, that the love of Christ
will gather them into the fellowship of the saints ...
May they rejoice in your heavenly feast where he pre-
sides for ever.

May the Lord receive our offering of prayer and multi-
ply it towards the coming of his Kingdom.

PROPER 13

Let us pray to the Father through whose Son we have
grace to do his will.

Bless your faithful people with the peace and unity
by which we are sealed in the Spirit ... Empower the
ministers of your Church, that they may bring the true
bread of life to all who seek.

Grant to a troubled world the stability and firmness of
purpose that only you can bring ... Reveal your will to
each member of your human creation, that all may serve
you according to the gifts that you have given.

Give grace to us, our families and friends, that in our
words and deeds we may show the sincerity of our
faith ... Make us pure in our motives, never looking
for material benefit when we are called to work in
your service.

Have mercy on those who seek you in ignorance, not
knowing the reality of their search ... Satisfy their
hunger and thirst for salvation.

May Jesus Christ, who descended into the depths to
bring new life to all, receive the souls of the departed

... We pray that the bread of heaven shall feed them evermore.

Trusting in Christ, the true and living bread, we offer our prayers in his name.

PROPER 14

Let us pray to the Father through the Son in whom he has been revealed.

Cleanse the Church from all malice and dissension ... Grant to your people the unity of purpose that will spread peace to others ... Give to those you have called to your service grace to be ministers of the bread of life.

Look with compassion on the world where anger so often prevails over love, where false speech and evil words destroy human fellowship ... Make all know the peace that is in Christ through his death for the life of the world.

In all our words, to families and friends, to neighbours and colleagues, help us to speak gently and with understanding ... Bring reconciliation wherever in this community fellowship has been broken.

Have mercy on those whose lives are twisted by bitterness ... All who cannot forgive others or cannot find freedom from personal guilt ... Relieve them with the knowledge of redeeming love.

According to your promise, grant eternal life to those who have died in the faith of Christ ... As they were strengthened by the bread of life in this world, grant them everlasting refreshment in your heavenly Kingdom.

We pray through Christ who has called us to himself and will raise us up to eternal life.

PROPER 15

As we prepare to receive the spiritual food of the Eucharist, let us pray to the Lord.

Fill the Church with divine wisdom, that your people may walk in the way of truth and peace ... Give us always the grace of your holy sacraments and bless those who administer them.

Pardon the folly which the world thinks to be wisdom ... Reveal the errors that bring wrong decisions and cause suffering ... Give right judgement to all in authority.

Guide us, our families and friends, to live according to your will ... May they live in Christ as he and the Father are one.

Have mercy on all who are enslaved by addiction ... Free them from their dependence and draw them to yourself to receive the healing power of your sacrament.

We give thanks for all who, having praised your name in the world, now join in the eternal adoration of heaven ... Have mercy on those who are dying and grant them the comfort of holy communion at their end.

May we who receive the Body and Blood of Christ be heard as we pray in his name.

PROPER 16

Let us pray to the Father who sent the Son to be the Saviour of the world.

Protect the Church with the whole armour of faith and righteousness ... Strong in the Spirit, may your people

work powerfully for the coming of your Kingdom ...
Keep us firm in loyalty to Christ, the Word of eternal
life.

Bring peace to the many places of strife in the world
... Turn the hearts of those who take the weapons of
destruction, and give them a truer vision ... Bless all
who work for peace.

Grant to our families the security that can come only
from faith ... Bless us, our friends and neighbours,
and be our sure defence against all evil.

Pity and pardon those who have lost the faith which
they once held ... Come to them with the assurance
that, though they have forsaken you, you will never
forsake them and will bring them home.

We give thanks for those who, having come to the
Father through the Son, have entered into eternal life
... Give them rest and peace now that the warfare of
this world is over for them.

In the strength of this holy sacrament, we offer these
our prayers.

PROPER 17

Let us pray to the Lord, who knows all the secrets of
our hearts.

Give grace to the Church to be steadfast in faith, firm
in your word, zealous in good work ... Keep your
people strong when their discipleship is costly and the
burden is heavy.

Have mercy on your human creation that does not
recognise its true identity ... Restore the world to
knowledge of the truth and lead it out of the slavery
of error into the perfect law of liberty.

Fill us with praise for the good gifts that you have given to us in families and friendships . . . Give us grace to use them in your service for the good of others.

Visit and relieve all who suffer from cruelty and injustice under evil laws . . . Through the sufferings of Christ, grant them release and turn the hearts of their persecutors.

We give thanks for the peace of the departed, whose suffering is over and who rest in your care . . . Grant them a place in the glory of heaven.

We pray that our petitions may be pure and acceptable in the sight of God.

PROPER 18

Let us pray to God whose love embraces all that he has made.

Grant to your whole Church grace to show true faith through works of love and mercy . . . Take away all prejudice that causes unequal treatment . . . May the places where your name is honoured be always open and welcoming to all who come.

Have compassion on a world where rich and poor are separated by selfishness and lack of understanding . . . Inspire those who are rich in this world's goods to respond to the necessity of individuals and nations . . . Bless all who work for the relief of poverty.

We pray that we, our families and friends, may have ears open to hear your word and tongues eager to make it known . . . Make us sensitive to discern the needs in our community and generous to relieve them.

We pray for the sick, especially for sick children and those who grieve for them . . . Have mercy on those who are afflicted in speech or hearing, and restore them to full power.

As we pray for the departed, we remember those who suffered from any impairment of faculties in this life, and are now made perfect in your love ... We pray too for those whose hearts were hard, that they may be pardoned through the saving mercy of Christ.

That we may be worthy to receive the true bread, we pray in the name of Christ.

PROPER 19

Let us pray to the Father, who has called us to follow Christ in all things.

Empower your Church to follow Christ in all things, courageous to face the hard demands of the Gospel ... Keep your people from idle gossip and evil speaking, that the purity of their witness shall not be corrupted.

Fill with the love of truth those who influence the minds of others ... Give to journalists and broadcasters the desire to make known the good as well as the bad, and to avoid anything than can mislead the innocent.

We pray for all who are suffering from slander and false accusations ... For those unjustly accused through malice or error ... Give courage to those who are called to witness to their faith in peril and persecution.

Guard our speaking as we meet with others ... Shield us in our families and in all our relationships from hasty words and disregard of truth.

We pray that the souls of the departed who loved this world too much may be pardoned in the Kingdom where true joys are to be found . . . May no evil report harm the memory of those who are at rest.

As those who trust in Christ, the true Messiah, we pray in his name.

PROPER 20

Let us pray to the Father whose Son suffered betrayal and death for the salvation of the world.

Cleanse the Church from temptation to worldly ambition and false triumphalism . . . In childlike simplicity, may your people follow you without fear, in loving one another.

Bring peace to the troubled places of the world, where war destroys both human life and the beauty of your creation . . . Make peaceful the minds of those who contend for power, that they may know the freedom of your service.

Bless the children of our families and those in our community . . . Let their innocence teach us to avoid all that may destroy the harmony of living.

Have mercy on the victims of war and violence . . . Those who have lost their loved ones and been driven from their homes . . . Grant them a place of refuge to rebuild their lives.

We pray for those who have died in war or through human violence . . . Grant mercy to those who died unprepared and impenitent, by the love of Christ who served others even to death . . . Grant them the peace that they were denied in their last hour.

As servants of Christ, we humbly offer our prayers in his name.

PROPER 21

Let us pray to the Lord who calls us to follow him in holiness of life.

Cleanse the Church from all that may hinder the spread of the Gospel . . . Give wisdom to discern where there is offence, and grace to set it right . . . Make your people strong in the power of prayer.

Give grace to all who work for good in the world and do not know that they are in your service . . . Enlighten them with the perfect knowledge of your majesty and with power to cast out evil and promote your Kingdom.

Strengthen us in prayer, so that we may in our families and in all our lives be sustained by your continual presence . . . Guide us as we intercede for those known to us who are distressed and afflicted.

Comfort and relieve the sick, especially those who have asked for our prayers . . . Bless the Church's ministry of healing . . . Grant perseverance to all who have become discouraged in prayer.

Accept the prayers which we offer for those who have died . . . Though we see them no longer, unite us with them in our intercessions, that we may be one in your love.

We pray as those who seek to be faithful members of the Kingdom of God.

PROPER 22

Let us pray to God, who from the beginning has made all things for his loving purpose.

Grant to the Church grace to witness unceasingly to Jesus Christ her Lord ... Empower your ministers to proclaim his lordship and the coming of his Kingdom.

Bless and keep all children ... May they grow in health of mind and body, learning to live in the way of love and faith ... Grant them the loving care that will support them into happy and secure lives.

We pray for our families, and for all the families in this community ... Protect and guide them day by day, as they look to you in faith for all their needs ... Strengthen our love when we are together and when we are apart.

Have mercy on those whose marriages are broken or under great strain ... Grant healing in the restoration of love that has been lost ... Tenderly comfort the children of broken homes.

We give thanks for the departed who have been brought to glory by the power of Christ ... Grant them rest and peace in the family of heaven where all are for ever one in him.

As little children, may we pray in faith and simplicity.

PROPER 23

Let us pray to God, in whose love and power all things are possible.

Keep your Church holy, free from desire for earthly wealth and glory ... Make your preachers powerful to proclaim your saving word ... Guide all who confess your name, that they may walk in the way of your commandments.

Have mercy on all whose wealth in this world holds them back from the knowledge of where true riches are found ... Inspire the rulers of wealthy nations to feel compassion for those that are poor ... In your mercy, do not send the rich empty away.

Bless us, our families and friends, with desire truly to follow you ... Shield us from all temptation, in the strength of Jesus Christ who was tempted like us but lived a fully human life on earth without sin.

We pray for those who have heard your call but failed to follow you ... For those who have been unable to fulfil their vocations or have lost their first desire ... Grant wisdom and love to those who guide others to find the right way.

Grant the inheritance of eternal life to those who have followed you here ... Receive them in mercy as they come to your presence, and look upon the image in them of their great High Priest who has passed before them into heaven.

We pray in the name of Christ who has made us inheritors of eternal life.

PROPER 24

Let us pray to the Father, who sent the Son to be a ransom for many.

Bless those whom you have called to be priests and ministers in the Church ... Fulfil your purpose in them, that they may always be faithful to the divine priesthood of Christ ... Free them from worldly ambition and guide them to serve you faithfully in all things.

Give to the rulers of the world that wisdom and care that can come only from your grace ... Let all in authority use their positions with justice, learning that the spirit of service is greater than the love of power.

In our homes and in our work, shield us from selfish disputes . . . With mutual love, let us live in the obedience that Jesus taught his followers by his word and his example.

Have mercy on those who suffer under oppressive power . . . Strengthen those who are sad and afflicted . . . Heal their suffering through the sufferings of Christ.

We pray that the departed may rest in Christ, the author of their salvation . . . Have mercy on those who are dying, that as they share his experience of death, they may rise with him to eternal life.

We offer our prayers through Christ, as his loving servants.

PROPER 25

Let us pray to God for a clear vision of his everlasting truth.

Bless your Church with grace faithfully to offer the sacrifices of praise and worship due to your name . . . Inspire your people to play their part in the priesthood of all believers, for the greater glory of the Kingdom.

Have pity on the world where so many stumble in the darkness of suspicion and prejudice . . . Open the eyes of the ignorant and direct them into the way of truth . . . Hear the voices of those who cry out for your mercy.

Unite us, our families and friends and neighbours, in sharing the vision of your glory . . . Make us quick to discern the needs of the handicapped in our community and eager to help them.

Have mercy on all who are afflicted with loss or imperfection of sight . . . Shield them as they walk and travel . . . Strengthen them with your inner light . . . Bless and enable the work of eye surgeons and all who seek to relieve the needs of the blind.

We commend the souls of the departed, confident in the interceding mercy of Christ, who will save to the uttermost . . . Grant them the perpetual vision of your glory.

We ask that our prayers will lead us to follow in the way of Christ.

or BIBLE SUNDAY

As Year A, p. 49.

DEDICATION FESTIVAL

As Year A, p. 50.

ALL SAINTS' SUNDAY

As Year A, p. 51.

FOURTH SUNDAY BEFORE ADVENT

Let us pray to God, with wholehearted love for him and for all people.

Grant that the Church, always remembering the great commandments, may worship you in love, and reveal her faith by showing love to all . . . May your people serve you, the living God, in word and deed.

Fill the world with knowledge of the divine love without which nothing is blessed and the human love without which none can be whole . . . Make the rulers and the lawgivers obedient to your law.

Give us true love every day, to live as knowing all to be our neighbours . . . Bless our children and enable us to lead them into the way of love.

Have mercy on those who feel themselves to be unloved and unwanted . . . Give them the comfort of your presence . . . Turn and soften those whose hearts are hardened against their neighbours.

May the sacrifice of Christ avail for the salvation of the departed . . . We pray for those we have loved here on earth and who have entered into rest.

That our prayers may be made perfect in love, we offer them through Christ our Lord.

THIRD SUNDAY BEFORE ADVENT

Let us pray to God, that his Kingdom may come and his Gospel be proclaimed.

Give to the Church the spirit of sincere repentance, so that she may be fit to preach repentance to the world . . . Enable your people both to follow you faithfully and to draw others to faith.

Come into the towns and cities, the crowded places where people live with stress . . . Break the darkness of ignorance and indifference with the sorrow for sin that brings your pardon.

In our daily work, let us always know that you are near, so that we may be ready to hear your call . . . Bless those with whom we work, and show them your salvation.

We pray for the lonely ones, who have lost the families that they once knew ... Be near to those whose work sends them into places far from home, holding them in continuing love for one another.

Have mercy on the departed, for whom Christ suffered that they might live for ever ... Remembering that all must die and enter into judgement, grant us repentance and renewal while we are still in this world.

As Christ has called us to his service, we pray in his name.

SECOND SUNDAY BEFORE ADVENT

Let us pray for the peace of God in the Church and among the nations.

As your people come together for worship, fill them with your love and keep them faithful in that holy fellowship ... Protect the Church from false doctrine and all that is contrary to your word.

Give to the world freedom from war and fear of war ... Grant true judgement where there is injustice ... Let all human endeavour that is wasted in limited aims be turned to your eternal purpose.

Protect this community from all false rumours and damaging gossip ... Grant to us, our families, friends and neighbours, the full assurance of faith.

We pray for those who suffer from war and live in fear of violence ... Have mercy on the victims of famine and natural disasters, and give strength to those who work for their relief.

We pray for all who have died and come to judgement, that in your mercy they may receive everlasting life

. . . May the Blood of Christ make them clean from all their sins.

Trusting in Christ, the one true Messiah, we pray in his name.

CHRIST THE KING

Let us pray to the Lord, King of all things on earth and in heaven.

Grant that the Church always rejoice in you, her heavenly King . . . Make all your people true priests to serve for your greater glory, to inherit a Kingdom that is not of this world.

Bless those who rule the nations and all who have authority over others . . . Make them know that true kingship is yours alone . . . Grant them wisdom in governing, so that justice and peace may everywhere prevail.

Give us grace to witness for the truth to all those among whom we live and work . . . Protect in your love our families and friends and deliver them from evil.

Have mercy on all who have fallen into the power of cruel and unjust authority . . . Give them courage and patience in their suffering, and guidance to answer when they are falsely accused.

May the saving power of Christ, the first-begotten from the dead, bring the faithful departed to eternal life . . . Grant them the vision of glory which no mortal eye can fully see.

Obedient to Christ, our heavenly King, we pray in his name.

Principal Service

Year C

FIRST SUNDAY OF ADVENT

As we look for the coming of the Kingdom, let us pray to the Lord.

Grant that the Church, filled with fervent love for you and for all that you have made, may grow in holiness and in your service . . . Teach us to look for the signs of your will and to be always ready for your calling.

Cleanse the world of selfish indulgence and the excesses that make people deaf to your word . . . Bless all nations, that they may be governed with true judgement and righteous dealing.

Fill us, in our families and friendships, with love for one another . . . Keep us faithful in prayer, when we are together and when we are apart.

Have mercy on all who are enslaved by any kind of addiction . . . Set them free and heal the damage they have done to themselves and others . . . Bless the work of those who work for the recovery of addicts.

We pray for those who have been called from this world, that they may be numbered with your saints . . . Keep us always mindful that we too await the same call, and make us ready to stand in your fuller presence.

With hearts and minds open to the call of Christ, we pray in his name.

SECOND SUNDAY OF ADVENT

Let us pray to the Lord for the word of salvation to be made known to all people.

Strengthen your faithful people as messengers and ministers of your word, that all may hear and believe ... Confirm our fellowship in the Gospel and keep us constant in truth until the coming of Christ.

Make straight the crooked ways of the world where people stumble without guidance, and make smooth the rough places where life is hard ... Come with your power to bring joy to the nations and knowledge of salvation to all people.

Give grace to us, our families and friends, to live together in love and to desire all that is good ... Cleanse us from all that holds us back from you.

Have mercy on all who are held so fast by sin that they cannot repent ... Grant them the true sense of your mercy and the good news of forgiveness ... Free those who cannot forgive themselves, and give them confidence in your redeeming love.

We pray for the departed whose fellowship is now complete in you ... Grant them salvation in the spirit after the death of the flesh.

Repenting of our sins and trusting in the mercy of Christ, we make our prayers through him.

THIRD SUNDAY OF ADVENT

Let us pray that the whole world may be led into the way of righteousness.

Gather into one body your Church that is scattered in different places and separated groups ... Unite us, that we may rejoice together that we share in your salvation . . . Grant sincere repentance for the faults in each that has held us apart.

Move with compassion those who use the power of authority or of money to exploit others . . . Lead those who rule the rich nations of the world to bring relief to the poor.

Make us just in all our dealings, with those among whom we live and those with whom we work . . . Grant that we shall hold fast and honour all that is good and beautiful.

Have mercy on refugees who have been torn from their homes to seek new lands . . . Relieve the afflicted and sorrowful who feel that they have no place in the world, and give them new hope.

We give thanks for those who have died in faith and rejoice in your presence . . . Grant them the eternal peace that passes all understanding.

May the grace of Christ enable us to bring forth fruits worthy of repentance.

FOURTH SUNDAY OF ADVENT

Let us pray to the Lord, rejoicing that he is here among us.

Make the Church, confident in the sacrifice of Christ, always ready to proclaim his coming . . . Keep your people faithful to the revelation that they have received, that they may be blessed in believing and ready to receive your promises.

Establish your justice in the world . . . In this winter time, give to the nations the light of Christ, that they may rejoice in his birth ... Let your will be known and followed by all people.

Bless us in our families with mutual love and service, to meet each other's needs ... Make us holy in our lives together as we wait for the holy birth.

Fill the hungry and raise up the oppressed ... Affirm the minorities that are despised because they are small and weak in the eyes of the world, and grant them their rightful place.

We pray for those who through bodily death have known the coming of the Lord ... May they be held in eternal life through his offering of himself.

May we be filled with the Holy Spirit, to make known the wonderful coming of Christ.

CHRISTMAS DAY

As Year A, p. 4.

FIRST SUNDAY OF CHRISTMAS

In the house of God our Father, let us pray to him for the Church and for the world.

Grant to all Christian people the spirit of forgiving and reconciling love, for mutual support and for a clear witness to the world ... Bless with wisdom those who are called to teach and expound your word.

We pray for the children in many parts of the word who are in need ... Nourish those who are hungry for food or for love ... Strengthen and enable all who work to relieve child poverty and neglect.

We pray for the children of our own families and all

who live in our community ... Guide all parents and teachers, that our children may grow up in health of body, mind and spirit.

Have mercy on families that are broken and divided ... Comfort parents who seek for children who are lost or alienated from them, and restore them in safety and love.

We give thanks for the lives of the departed who have enriched others by their love ... Grant them reunion with those they have loved, to share with them in your eternal joy.

As we seek in our prayers the will of Christ, may we have grace always to find him.

SECOND SUNDAY OF CHRISTMAS

Let us pray to the Father who sent his Son to live on earth and make us children of God.

Grant that your Church, blessed with the knowledge of the Word made flesh, may faithfully proclaim the good news of the redemption which he brought ... As we are called to your service, guide and enable us to fulfil the tasks which are your will for us.

Have pity on all in the world who still do not know and receive the faith of Christ ... Through his power, make light the dark places, so that all peoples and nations may be gathered into one.

Bless us, our families and friends, with the grace and peace of Christ ... Make our homes fit places for those who are called to be your children, adopted in him.

Have mercy on those who deny you because they trust their own strength and have not opened their hearts to your grace ... Come to those who are not at peace with themselves, and comfort them with the peace of your presence.

We pray for those who, born again by grace in this world, have passed through the new birth to eternal life ... Hold them in the peace that was prepared for them from the beginning.

We pray through Christ our Lord from whom we have received grace upon grace.

THE EPIPHANY

As for Year A, p. 7.

THE BAPTISM OF CHRIST

That the Church and all the world may be cleansed and sanctified, let us pray to the Lord.

Fill your Church with the Holy Spirit, that all who respond to your call may be witnesses to your name ... Bless those who come to be baptised and those who stand as their godparents or sponsors.

Come with power to the world, to make your name known and honoured in every place ... Guide those you have chosen to be your agents in places of authority, that they may rule with justice and break down all barriers to the truth.

Bless our families with your presence, helping us so to live that what we do shall be pleasing to you ... Bless all parents in this community, and grant that they may bring up their children in faith and obedience to your word.

Have mercy on those who suffer persecution for confessing your name ... Pardon those who use their power to act against human rights . . . Open their eyes to see the way of love.

Receive with mercy the souls of those who have died in the faith of Christ . . . Open the Kingdom of Heaven to them that they may enter into eternal life.

We offer our prayers through Christ the Son, the Beloved.

SECOND SUNDAY OF EPIPHANY

Let us pray to the Lord, the bountiful giver of love and mercy.

Give grace to the Church, to be a crown of glory and a sign to the world . . . Guide your people to discern the special gifts that you have given to each and to use them fully in your service.

Grant that all skill and wisdom may be rightly used for the advancement of your Kingdom . . . Take away human pride, and give understanding that all gifts come from you.

We pray that in our families we may so live that we know you are always among us . . . Bless all in our community who are recently married or soon to marry, that they may hold together in love and loyalty all their lives.

Have mercy on those who suffer in unhappy marriages, on those who are separated or divorced . . . Bring healing and reconciliation where marriages are in danger, that love may be restored and promises fulfilled.

As we pray for the departed, we remember with thanks all that they gave to the life of this world . . .

Grant them joy in the everlasting marriage feast of heaven.

We pray in the name of Christ, the mystical Bride-groom of his Church.

THIRD SUNDAY OF EPIPHANY

Let us pray that all the Lord's people may be anointed with his Spirit.

Keep the Church steadfast in observance of your law, to be a witness to all nations ... Guide and inspire all who are called to your service, enabling them to fulfil the different tasks entrusted to them.

Grant to all peoples of the earth the spirit of co-operation for the common good ... Teach us to use our resources for the relief of suffering and the spreading of peace and harmony.

Bless us in our families, to care for one another in the knowledge that we are one in Christ ... Inspire us to respect those with whom we work and to honour what they do.

Have mercy on all who suffer from poverty or sickness or any other distress ... Relieve their trouble, and comfort them with the word of your salvation.

We pray that those who have died in their earthly bodies may be made whole in the heavenly body of all the faithful ... Comfort those who mourn, with the good news that all are one in Christ.

We offer our prayers through Christ in whom all Scripture has been fulfilled.

FOURTH SUNDAY OF EPIPHANY

Let us pray to God who has prepared for us a wonderful salvation.

May our churches be filled with your glory, and may our worship be always acceptable in your sight ... Inspire your people with such true and unfailing love that they may draw together in unity and shine as a light to the world.

Come into the hearts of all with your transforming love, to break down the barriers that hold people apart ... Forgive the imperfections of human vision and bless the world with better knowledge of your greatness and love.

Bless our families and guide us to fulfil in our lives your command of love ... Shield from harm the children of our community, giving love and wisdom to their parents and all who care for them.

Have pity on those whose hearts are hardened by pride and envy so that they have forgotten how to love ... Come to those who feel unloved and unwanted and give them understanding of their worth as your children.

We give thanks for the love that brings life out of death ... Grant to the departed the perfect sight of your everlasting glory.

As we end our prayers may they be received in the peace of Christ.

THE PRESENTATION OF CHRIST

As Year A, p. 11.

ORDINARY TIME

PROPER 1

Let us pray to God, who gives more abundantly than we dare to ask.

Grant that the Church, confident in the power of the Resurrection, shall be always alert to hear your call and faithful to follow it ... Give your people courage to launch out into the deep and make your word known to all.

Give to the world a new vision of your glory ... Raise up witnesses who in your name will turn the hearts of men and women from hostility to friendship and from suspicion to trust.

In all our work, strengthen us to co-operate with others for the common good ... Bless our families, friends and neighbours with the joy of knowing the Risen Christ.

Have mercy on those who are weary and discouraged because they see no result for their work ... Strengthen them to persevere and to trust in your calling.

We pray for those who have died and have been raised to new life ... Grant them the eternal glory which Christ won for them by his saving death for our sins.

As sinners, we pray in the name of Christ that he will not reject us for our sins.

PROPER 2

For his blessings on all that he has made, let us pray to the Lord.

Strengthen the Church to flourish like a tree planted by the water, bringing forth fruit to the glory of your Kingdom ... Keep your people steadfast in trouble, always trusting in your promises.

Change and heal the inequalities and injustices of the world ... Guide the rich that they may help the poor, and the well fed that they may relieve the hungry ... Teach the powerful not to trust in their own strength but only in your love.

We pray for grace that we, our families and friends and neighbours, may hear and receive your word and walk in your way ... Make us more worthy to be members of your Kingdom.

Grant healing to the sick in body or mind and empower those who minister to them ... Be with those who are near to death and give them the assurance of resurrection.

Receive the souls of the faithful by the power of Christ, the firstfruits of those who have passed through death ... Confirm our hope in him when we come to die.

We offer our prayers as those who come to Christ that they may be healed.

PROPER 3

Let us pray to the Father, whose pardoning love embraces all people.

Grant that the Church, trusting in Christ, the Second Adam, may proclaim with confidence the good news of redemption ... Give your people grace to be patient and forgiving, seeking to be in love and peace with all.

Look with pity on the anger and violence of the world ... Bring peace between nations ... Grant to all who are at variance with each other the will to forgive wrongs and live in harmony.

We pray that our families may always be kept in perfect love and care for one another ... Give us grace to be peacemakers when there is strife among those with whom we live and work.

Have mercy on families that are broken by resentment and misunderstanding ... Bring them reconciliation in the power of your love.

We pray for those who have died and are changed from mortality to immortality by the power of the Risen Christ ... Give them joy in your heavenly Kingdom.

That we may love others as Christ loves us, we pray in his name.

SECOND SUNDAY BEFORE LENT

Let us pray for the peace of God in the Church and in the world.

Fill the Church with adoration of your glory, to worship you with reverence and wonder ... Bless your people, giving them courage to hold fast in faith when the storms of life arise.

Help us to honour all that you have created ... Guide all people to live responsibly towards the natural world ... Grant that men and women may live with mutual respect, honouring one another for the sake of your image in them.

Bless our families with obedience to follow your will ... Open our eyes to see the signs of your glory in our daily lives.

Have mercy on those who are in danger from storms and other disturbances of nature ... Keep them safe and give them the calm of your presence ... Be with members of the rescue services and protect them in their work.

We pray for those who have passed through the perils of life and are safe in your care ... Grant them a share in the everlasting worship offered by the hosts of heaven.

Trusting in Christ that we shall not perish in the storms of life, we pray in his name.

SUNDAY BEFORE LENT

Let us pray to the Father who has revealed his glory through his Son.

We pray that the Church, bearing your image before the world, may be changed from glory to glory towards the coming of your Kingdom ... Make your people worthy ministers of the riches of the Gospel.

Grant to the world the sight of your glory ... Come to those whose vision is veiled by material cares, and give them light.

Give grace to us, our families, friends and neighbours, to find you in the daily events of life ... Be present with us when we are alone and when we are with others.

Have mercy on those who know you only imperfectly and do not serve you as they should ... Pardon their blindness and give them the full light of salvation.

We pray for those who have passed through the veil of death to behold your glory ... Grant them peace in the perfection of the blessed.

Rejoicing that it is good for us to be here, we make our prayers through Christ the Lord.

ASH WEDNESDAY

As Year A, p. 16.

FIRST SUNDAY OF LENT

Let us pray to the Father, who through the Son has shown us the way of righteousness.

Grant that the Church, confessing the faith of the Lord Jesus, shall never cease to praise you for your mercies ... Give to your people strength to resist temptation and to acknowledge you, the only God.

Bless the earth that it may give food for our needs ... Prosper the work of those who produce and distribute food ... Bring relief to those who live in barren places and struggle for existence.

Bless our families and friends with stability in our homes and sufficiency for our needs ... Keep us in harmony with our neighbours and those with whom we work, making us free from all that seems to divide us.

Have mercy on those who lack the means of life ... Deliver from evil all men and women who feel temptation, and show them the way of righteousness.

We give thanks for the faithful departed, who in their lives confessed Jesus as Lord ... By his rising from the dead, grant them eternal life.

Strengthened by the example of Christ, we pray that we may be saved from all sin.

SECOND SUNDAY OF LENT

Let us pray to the Father whose Son died and rose on the third day for our salvation.

Keep your Church steadfast in faith, trusting in the cross of Christ ... May we always rest under your protection and be ready for your coming in glory.

Have mercy on the world where so many follow their selfish ways and seek false goals ... Enlighten them and bring them to knowledge of the truth.

Grant us perfect trust in your promises for our families and all whom we love ... Free us from anxiety for the future ... In all our relationships grant us the fellowship that is in Christ.

Have mercy on those who are persecuted for their witness to the truth ... Give them courage and turn the hearts of those who treat them unjustly.

Receive the souls of the departed, changing their mortal bodies into the glorious bodies of resurrection ... May they rest in peace and rise in glory.

Rejoicing that we are gathered safely in the love of Christ, we make our prayers through him.

THIRD SUNDAY OF LENT

Let us pray for the good fruits of God's love.

Save the Church from becoming slothful and complacent ... Keep us mindful of judgement while we rejoice in mercy ... Free your people from the sins that would separate them from you.

Bless the nations with thirst for the healing waters of your love ... Teach us to guard against waste of the riches you have given to the earth, and strengthen our resolve to bring relief where there is human need.

Give grace to us, our families and friends, to resist temptation and stand firm in the power of faith ...

Bless us in our work, so that we may seek goals that will bring benefit to others.

Have mercy on the victims of disasters across the world ... Visit and relieve those who suffer from human cruelty, and make merciful the hearts of oppressors.

We pray for those who have died suddenly and unprepared ... Grant them pardon for their sins, that they may rest in peace and be blessed with eternal life.

We pray that in Christ we may have time for repentance and newness of life.

FOURTH SUNDAY OF LENT

Let us pray to the Father who meets us in our need and receives us in his love.

Renew the Church in the faith of Christ, rejoicing in the new birth of our redemption ... We pray that through him your people shall be granted repentance and reconciliation.

Give to all the wisdom to make good use of your gifts and the grace to be thankful for them ... Where there has been offence and separation between nations and races, bring the desire to forgive what is past and live in peace.

In our families and in all our lives, grant us the spirit of true forgiveness and reconciliation ... Correct us when we go astray, and help us to live in love and harmony with all.

We pray for all who have separated themselves from those they love ... We pray for those whose own folly has brought them into want ... Restore them and bring them back to the life that they have lost.

Have mercy on the departed, not condemning them for their sins but receiving them into the perfect life that is in Christ ... Grant peace to the living who grieve because they feel unreconciled with any who have died.

As sinners who have strayed and seek to be forgiven, we pray through Christ our Saviour.

or **MOTHERING SUNDAY** see p. 158.

FIFTH SUNDAY OF LENT

Let us pray to God with the reverence and honour due to his name.

May the Church, created for your service, always have grace to praise you and glorify your name ... Keep your people both faithful to the teaching they have received and also open to follow new ways that may be your will for them.

May your power be honoured through your creatures as people learn to respect all that you have made ... Be with those who are entrusted with financial responsibility, keeping them honest and open in all their dealings.

Bless us, our families and friends, that we may be committed to those with whom we live but never forget the loyalty that is due to you alone ... Guide us to remember the poor in our community and to show our love for you through love for them.

Have mercy on those who are victims of their own failures to love ... Give them the spirit of true generosity towards others ... Have mercy on all who suffer from the meanness and injustice of those who should provide for them.

We pray for those who have died, that they may have

eternal life through the power of Christ's resurrection ... May they rest in his love and rise in his glory.

That our prayers may be worthy to be received, we offer them in the name of Christ.

PALM SUNDAY

As Year A, p. 21.

MAUNDY THURSDAY

As Year A, p. 22.

GOOD FRIDAY

As Year A, p. 23.

EASTER EVE

As Year A, p. 24.

EASTER DAY

As Year A, p. 24.

SECOND SUNDAY OF EASTER

In the power of the Spirit, who works through all creation, let us pray to the Lord.

Bless the Church, created to witness to your name, and inspire her ministry of declaring your forgiveness ... As your people are made kings and priests by your grace, teach us the humility that belongs to our high calling, that we may give glory to you alone.

May the whole world acknowledge your power, as Ruler of all, the beginning and the end . . . Be merciful to those who find it hard to believe the good news, and grant them faith.

Make us witnesses to those with whom we live and work . . . Bless our families when we are gathered together and when we are apart.

Have mercy on the lonely who feel shut out from the company of others . . . Give them open hearts and the blessing of human fellowship.

Grant to the departed forgiveness of their sins . . . May they have eternal life in Christ, through his triumph over death.

We make our prayers in the name of Christ, revealed to us through the eyes of faith.

THIRD SUNDAY OF EASTER

In sincere love, let us pray to the Lord whose love has given us light and life.

Grant that the Church may always be fervent to proclaim your glory . . . In the power of the Resurrection, give your people grace to love you deeply and to follow you faithfully.

Fill the whole world with your power, that all may acknowledge you . . . Give light to those who are in the darkness of ignorance and prejudice . . . Let all men and women know the particular calling that is your purpose for them.

Give grace to us, our families and friends, to recognise

the presence of Christ in all we do ... In our lives together, make us witnesses to the love that he brings to all who will follow him.

Have mercy on all who are grieved with guilt because they have wronged any that they loved ... Restore the broken relationships and heal the wounds of past betrayals.

We pray for those who have died, that they may have life in Christ ... Bring them to the joy of heaven where they may worship and adore you for ever.

Responding to the call of Christ that we should follow him, we pray in his name.

FOURTH SUNDAY OF EASTER

Let us pray to God, the loving Shepherd of the Church and of all the world.

Grant that the Church, serving you in all good works, may bear witness to the Gospel of hope ... May Christ the Good Shepherd keep his people free from sin and safe from danger.

Bless all who work for the relief of poverty and need ... Open the hearts of the rich and powerful to give their help ... Teach us all to remember that we can do no good thing without your grace.

Bless us in our families and in our work, that we shall always be ready to hear your voice and follow your commands ... Keep us faithful to the fellowship of love in which we are called to be your own.

Have mercy on all who are in any kind of tribulation and distress ... Bring them the peace of your presence, relieve their suffering and wipe away all tears from their eyes.

Grant to the departed the vision of your glory and eternal life in the blessed company of heaven . . . Have mercy on all who mourn, and comfort them with assurance of resurrection and the ending of sorrow.

We pray in the name of Christ, that we may hear his voice and follow him.

FIFTH SUNDAY OF EASTER

Let us pray to the Lord, whose love commands us to love one another.

Give to the Church the spirit of holiness, to be the image here on earth of the New Jerusalem . . . Inspire your people with mutual love, so that all may know that we are your disciples.

Break through the prejudices that divide people from one another . . . Open the eyes of the proud, to see the worth of those they have despised . . . Give peace between nations and harmony between races.

Grant that in our families and in our friendships we shall truly love one another . . . In our work, and with our neighbours, keep us open to hear different opinions and to respect those with whom we disagree.

Comfort those who are outcast and unloved . . . Have mercy on all who suffer discrimination as members of minorities . . . Give grace to all who work for better understanding in places of racial or religious tension.

We pray for the departed, who have entered into new life . . . Keep them eternally where there is no more death, no sorrow or crying or pain.

As we pray in the name of Christ, may we ever be faithful to him.

SIXTH SUNDAY OF EASTER

In peace and confidence, let us pray to the Lord.

Make your Church a worthy temple for your presence ... Bless all missionaries and inspire them both with zeal for the Gospel and understanding of those to whom they preach.

Lighten the darkness of the world with the light of Christ ... Give the water of life to all who thirst for hope and direction in their human journey.

Grant that we and all those we love shall always be ready to respond to your call, to help each other or those as yet unknown to us ... Bless those in our community who have recently come to faith and strengthen them to grow in love and obedience day by day.

Bring healing to those who are sick in body or mind ... Lift up those whose spirits are weary ... Comfort those who mourn.

Grant to the faithful departed that they shall indeed see the face of Christ and live with him for ever ... May perpetual light shine upon them.

Taught by the Holy Spirit, we pray through Christ our Saviour.

ASCENSION DAY

As Year A, p. 29.

SEVENTH SUNDAY OF EASTER

Let us pray to the Lord, who calls us to be one in him and with him.

Grant to the Church the unity that is your will ...
Make us one with each other, that we may be made
perfect in you, the first and the last ... Empower us
to bring to others the water of life.

May the whole world know your love and see your
glory ... Give light to those who are in error and
follow the ways that lead to darkness ... Bring all
people into the gates of your Kingdom.

As we know ourselves loved in Christ, give us the
same love for our families and friends and neighbours
... Bless all in our community who are coming closer
to you and lead them into the fullness of faith.

Have mercy on all who are in captivity ... Give them
hope for the future and show them the way to new
lives ... Grant compassion to those who control the
lives of prisoners.

Receive the souls of the departed into the life of heaven
... Give them rest and peace, in perfect union with
Christ.

We make our prayers through Christ, that we may be
with him and see his glory.

PENTECOST

As Year A, p. 31.

ORDINARY TIME

TRINITY SUNDAY

As Year A, p. 32.

PROPER 4

Let us pray to God, the source of all authority and power.

Keep your Church faithful to the pure truth of the Gospel, resisting all false doctrine and human error ... Make all Christian people ministers of the word, bringing the blessing of peace to many.

Give to those in authority the wisdom to know that all power comes from you alone ... Fill them with compassion and a true desire to work for the good of those they govern ... May all men and women have the grace of respect for the sincere beliefs of others.

Give us grace to serve you through other people, in our homes and in our work ... Where we can command, teach us how to obey.

Have mercy on the sick in body or mind ... Bless doctors and nurses and all engaged in the work of healing, giving them confidence in your power to restore health and strength.

We pray for those who have recently died, that they shall rise again at your word ... Have mercy on all who are near to death and ease their passing to new life.

Unworthy of the presence of Christ, we offer our prayers through him, trusting in his love.

PROPER 5

Let us pray to God, whose compassion never fails and whose mercy is always new.

Fill the Church with knowledge of your glory, that your name may be proclaimed and honoured in all the world ... Give wisdom and fellowship to all church leaders.

Heal the divisions that arise from hostility between different faiths ... Grant greater understanding and the desire to live in peace with all.

Bless our families, and grant us loving concern for families that are in trouble ... Keep us firm in our faith but always tolerant to the opinions of those with whom we live and work.

Have mercy on all who mourn ... We pray especially for parents who have lost a child ... Be close to widows and widowers and comfort them in their need.

By the power of Christ who raised the dead, give eternal life to the departed ... We pray for those who have died young ... Give them peace, and grant that the good which was unfulfilled in their earthly lives may be carried through by others.

Confident in the new life that Christ gives to us, we make our prayers through him.

PROPER 6

Let us pray to God for mercy on the Church and on all people.

Sustain your Church with faith in the power of Christ ... Keep it free from the legalism that quenches the Spirit ... Grant to all Christian people the assurance that Christ lives in them.

Look with mercy on the world where injustice is often done in the name of law ... Fill all people with the spirit of generosity and openness to others ... Restore the outcast and despised to acceptance in their societies.

In our family life, keep us always ready to receive in your name those who need our love ... Give us the grace freely to forgive those who offend us in our work or social life.

Have mercy on all who are caught in debt that they cannot escape ... Help them in their need and grant mercy to their creditors ... Accept the sorrow of penitent sinners.

We pray for those who have died, that they may receive through the mercy of Christ forgiveness of sins and everlasting life ... May we in our time be saved through faith and depart in peace.

As sinners who know their need for mercy, we pray in the name of Christ.

PROPER 7

That the Church and the world may be cleansed from all evil, let us pray to the Lord.

As the Church has been shown the way of salvation through Christ alone, grant her perseverance in the faith which he taught ... Make her ministers strong in his word and empower them to bring release to those who are held under the tyranny of sin.

Grant to all people the understanding that they are your children, created to live together in peace ... May those who are in authority lead the way to breaking down false limits that keep races and nations apart.

Give to us, our families and friends, grace to receive with joy the signs of your presence, even when they disturb what is safe and familiar ... Give us compassion and understanding for all whose ways seem strange to us.

Come with your healing power to the mentally ill ... Grant them recovery and the way to a new life ... Bless and enable those who care for them.

Have mercy on those who have died with disturbed or confused minds, unable to respond to your love ... Give them rest in the perfect harmony of your heavenly Kingdom.

We pray through Christ who has restored us and made us whole.

PROPER 8

Let us pray to the Father who loves all races and nations of the world that he has made.

Bless the Church with growth in the pure liberty of the Gospel ... Raise up in this and every generation true ministers of the faith ... Grant that your people, walking in the Spirit, may be agents of love and peace to all.

Come to a world of much strife and envying, to set men and women free from all that makes them slaves of sin ... Give peace between nations, that the power of destruction may be turned to power for good.

Preserve us, our families, friends and neighbours from anger and disputes ... Let us live together in love and trust ... Keep us firm in the faith to which we have been called.

Have compassion on refugees and others who have lost their homes ... Be with all whose work brings them into dangerous and hostile places, and shield them from harm.

We commit to your mercy those who have died in the flesh, now to be united with Christ in the spirit ... Comfort those who mourn at this time for parents or other loved ones.

Looking ever forward in the service of Christ, we make our prayers through him.

PROPER 9

Let us pray to the Lord who has appointed us to serve him as his disciples in our time.

Keep the Church faithful, to trust only in the Cross of Christ ... Fill your people with love for one another and with zeal to spread the Gospel to all people.

Bless those who travel ... Keep them safe as they journey and guide them on their way ... Guide and protect all missionaries and bless those who support them.

Give us the grace of hospitality, that our homes shall be places of welcome ... Give us power to speak of the good news which we have received to those with whom we live and work.

Visit and relieve the homeless and the wanderers who have no place to rest ... Be merciful to all who find doors shut against them because society has rejected them ... Bless those who try to reach out to them in their need.

We pray for those who have come to the end of their earthly journey ... Receive them into their true home, to share the joy of the heavenly feast.

We pray in the name of Christ to be his faithful labourers.

PROPER 10

Let us pray to be made perfect in the love of God and of our neighbours.

May the Church, rejoicing in the redemption won by Christ, show herself worthy of her calling and be abundant in good work . . . Give to all clergy and lay ministers the grace both to be faithful in duty and compassionate to need.

Give light to this world where pressure of living too often leads to indifference and hardness of heart . . . Through the great commandment of love teach all to live as neighbours.

Make us and all in our families ready to serve those who need our help . . . Keep us alert and sensitive to signs of distress . . . Give strength to those in this community who care for the hurt and afflicted.

Have mercy on victims of crime and violence . . . Mend their brokenness and restore them to wholeness of life . . . Help those who support them in their trouble.

Receive the souls of the faithful into their inheritance of light . . . Deliver them from all evil and grant them rest in the Kingdom of Heaven.

We offer our broken and imperfect prayers to be transformed by the compassion of Christ.

PROPER 11

Let us pray to the Lord who through his word teaches us to pray.

Grant that the Church, the Body of Christ, may be in all things worthy of its Head . . . As we are reconciled through the Cross, make us reconcilers and messengers of his peace.

Be merciful to a world where so many are too concerned with the business of life to care for the things of the spirit . . . Give to those in places of authority the revelation of Christ as Lord of all, that he may rule in their hearts and direct their power into the way of love.

Give grace to us in our families to share the burdens of work and to be concerned for the needs of others . . . Give us the blessing of quietness, and time for recollection to be close to you.

Have mercy on all whose burden of work is heavy . . . Be with those who have no work, comfort their despair and guide them to find the employment that they desire.

We pray for the departed who rest from their labours . . . Grant them peace through the blood of the Cross. That we may always choose the better part, we pray in the name of Christ.

PROPER 12

As children of our heavenly Father, let us pray for the Church and for the world.

Guide your Church, rooted and grounded in Christ, in the way of the Gospel . . . As you have taught us to pray, keep us constant in prayer . . . Increase our faith, that we may bring our needs before you with perfect confidence.

Release all people from the selfishness of the closed door and the closed heart . . . Help them to care for the needs of others, knowing they are children of the same Father.

Give grace to us, our families, friends and neighbours, to be generous in giving . . . Teach us how to share our spiritual blessings and the good news of the Kingdom.

We pray for all those who feel excluded from the company of others . . . For those whose pleas for help in distress have been ignored . . . Give strength and perseverance to agencies of relief.

Receive the faithful departed who prayed on earth that their sins might be forgiven . . . As they were buried with Christ in baptism, may they rise with him to eternal life.

We make our prayer in the name of Christ, who has taught us how we should pray.

PROPER 13

Let us pray to God, who gives us the everlasting treasures of his love.

Keep your Church free from all that would harm her witness . . . Grant that all Christian people, being risen with Christ, may grow in holiness.

Break through the greed and complacency that are damaging the lives of many . . . Where there is strife for material possession, bring generosity and concern for the needs of others.

Keep us, our families and friends, in the way of peace, free from selfish quarrels . . . Make us more ready to share our good things with those in our community who are in need.

Have mercy on families divided by quarrels over inheritance and ownership . . . Bring healing where angry words and unjust deeds have separated those who should be close in love.

We pray for all who have died suddenly and unprepared ... Grant them pardon and peace through the power of the Resurrection.

We offer our prayers through Christ, that they may be pure and free from the taint of sin.

PROPER 14

Let us pray to the Father who in his love has given us the Kingdom.

Keep your Church steadfast in courage and in hope of the Kingdom ... Increase our faith so that we may follow the example of those who have faithfully served you through all the ages.

Look with pity on a world where many are anxious for the future and live in fear ... Grant to this generation the saving faith that has sustained your people in the past.

Bless us, our families and friends, with constancy in your service ... Make us always ready to know your power among us and to follow your call in ministry to others.

Have mercy on those who are sorrowful for the loss of things they valued ... Comfort them with the knowledge of the real treasure that lies in faith and give them strength in their trouble.

We commend into your gracious keeping all who have died in faith ... Grant them the fullness of your presence for which they lived continually in hope.

We pray in the name of Christ that we may be always ready to receive him.

PROPER 15

That we and all people may discern the time with wisdom, let us pray to the Lord.

Keep your Church faithful, ever looking to Jesus as her source and her goal ... As we serve you here on earth, let us always remember the witness of those who have gone before and who now support us with their prayers.

Give wisdom to men and women, to understand the needs of our time and to work for justice and peace ... May those who hold power and authority in the present be ready to learn from the wisdom of the past.

Give us grace in our families, and let each generation value what the others have to give ... Bless with love and harmony the families of our neighbours and those with whom we work.

Come with your healing power to broken and divided families ... Restore lost relationships and give patience to those that are threatened by difficulties.

We pray for those who have died after much suffering ... Grant them rest and peace in your heavenly Kingdom where there is no more pain and all sorrow is taken away.

We pray through Christ that we may rightly interpret and faithfully perform his will.

PROPER 16

Let us pray to God for the healing of the Church and the nations of the world.

Bless the Church, called to serve you here as the gathered people of your eternal purpose ... Empower us all as ministers of the new covenant, bringing hope and comfort to the world.

Be merciful to a world where so many turn away and will not hear your voice ... Lift us above the irreverence and contempt for holy things that mars your creation, and lead all people to acknowledge your power.

Rejoicing in your goodness to us, we pray for continuing grace for us, our families and all in our community ... Grant that we may be faithful in our religious duties, but let them never hold us back from works of mercy.

Have mercy on those who are afflicted with crippling and disabling diseases ... Give them patience in their suffering and grant them healing.

We give thanks for those who have come to the heavenly City ... Be merciful in their judgement and make them perfect in eternal life.

Made free by the love of Christ, we pray in his name.

PROPER 17

In penitence and humility, let us pray to the Lord.

Strengthen your Church in the assurance of Jesus Christ, the same yesterday, today and for ever ... May she continually offer through him the sacrifice of praise ... Keep your people in love and fellowship with one another, but always ready to receive and welcome strangers.

Come with power into the world where so many live in suspicion and distrust ... Heal the old hostilities that still divide races and nations ... Come to those who are proud in their power or wealth, and show them that all things are from you alone.

Bless us in our families with the grace of hospitality ... Keep us always open to those who call upon us for help, whoever they may be ... Give us good will towards all our neighbours.

Have mercy on those who are deprived and rejected through poverty or disability ... Help all who are working towards a more just society.

We give thanks for those who have died secure in the faith of Christ ... We pray too for those whose hearts were closed to him in this world, that they may receive mercy at the last.

We make our prayers through Christ, who has called us to share the eucharistic feast.

PROPER 18

For holy wisdom in the Church and in the world, let us pray to the Lord.

Keep the whole Church steadfast in faith, ready to bear the cost of discipleship ... May all Christian people honour one another in love, and give thanks for their redemption.

Look with compassion on the world where many strive to fulfil tasks that are too heavy for them ... Give wisdom to those who have power in disputes between nations, that they may count the cost of conflict before it is too late.

We pray that our human loves and loyalties may be blessed but never turn us from our spiritual duty ... Make us considerate to all who serve our daily needs.

Have mercy on those who are distressed because they

wrongly judged the consequences of what they desired to do ... We pray for all who have fled from their homes, that they may find support and the way of reconciliation.

We give thanks for those who have fulfilled their work on earth and entered into rest ... Grant them eternal life through the Cross that was borne for them.

We make our prayers through Christ who has called us to take up the Cross and follow him.

PROPER 19

Let us pray to God, by whose love all people are sustained and restored.

May Jesus the great Shepherd protect his flock the Church and lead back those who go astray ... Grant to your people true repentance and the joy of knowing forgiveness for their sins.

As the people of the world wander like sheep that are lost, guide them into the way of peace ... Grant the vision of your holiness to those who defame and seek to destroy the faith.

Give us grace to sympathise with our friends and neighbours in their sorrow and to rejoice with them in their joy ... Make us quick to discern troubles in our community and ready to relieve them.

Comfort those who are sad because one they love is far away from them ... Bless all who are lonely and away from home ... Keep them safe and bring them happy reunion with those they love.

Grant rest and peace to the dead, through the mercy of Christ who came into the world to save sinners ... Gather them into their true and eternal home.

As lost sheep brought back to the true fold, we pray through Christ our Shepherd.

PROPER 20

For the grace of faithful service to the Church and to the world, let us pray to the Lord.

May the Church be wise in all her ways without departing from holiness ... Sustain your people to be strong in prayer for the needs of the world.

We pray for those in authority, that they may lead the nations in peace and just government ... We pray that all who are entrusted with responsibility may be faithful and honourable in their work.

Bless our families with peaceful lives ... Keep us free from any failures of honesty in our work ... Give us the grace of integrity in all our relationships.

Have mercy on those who have suffered from the dishonesty of others ... Be with all who have lost their employment and feel in despair for the future.

As it is your will that all shall be saved and come to knowledge of the truth, have mercy on the departed ... Receive them in the love of Christ who gave himself as a ransom for many.

That we may be good stewards of Christ, we offer our prayers in his name.

PROPER 21

Let us pray to the God of compassion for light to know his will and grace to obey it.

Keep your Church alert to hear the message of salvation and eager to preach it . . . Grant to all Christian people the grace to make a good confession of their faith before the world.

In a world where a great gulf separates rich and poor, we pray for a new spirit of caring . . . Give to those who have authority in the rich nations the desire to aid nations that are in need.

Bless us, our families, friends and neighbours, with shared concern for our spiritual lives . . . Open our eyes to see the poor in our community and our hearts to give for their relief.

Have mercy on the destitute who have no shelter and no means of existence . . . Have mercy on the rich whose love of money has led them into evil ways and bring them back to know the true wealth of love for others.

We pray for the departed who have fought the good fight . . . Receive them into eternal life with all your saints . . . Grant to us who remain the time for repentance and more faithful lives.

For grateful hearts, open to the needs of others, we pray in the name of Christ.

PROPER 22

For increase of faith and the spirit of service, let us pray to the Lord.

Through the power of the Holy Spirit, keep the Church faithful to the teaching entrusted to her . . . Make your people obedient servants, seeking no reward but to do your will.

Grant to those in authority care and consideration for those who serve . . . Stir up in all people the knowledge of your gifts, that all may seek the good of others.

Bless us, our families and friends, with stronger faith ... Empower us to make known to our neighbours and those with whom we work the assurance which we have received.

Have mercy on all whose work is heavy and brings little reward ... Strengthen those who labour for the spread of the Gospel in difficulty and persecution.

We pray for those who have died, that they may find mercy through Jesus Christ who has destroyed death and brought new life ... Grant them rest from their labours.

As those who desire to be good servants of Christ, we offer our prayers in his name.

PROPER 23

Let us pray for the healing grace of God in the Church and in the world.

Keep your Church in the right way, to work for you without doubts or fears ... In your mercy grant that we shall never deny our Saviour but be bold to speak the words that he has taught us.

Come with your healing power to cleanse the world of prejudice against race or belief ... Inspire those who can relieve human need with the compassion that was in Jesus.

Give to us, our families, friends and neighbours, the spirit of gratitude for all the benefits we have received ... Bless those in our community who work for healing.

Have mercy on the sick, especially those who have long been ill and found no relief . . . Give them courage and perseverance and bring them new hope.

We pray that the departed, having shared bodily death with Christ, may share his resurrection . . . May they rest in peace and rise in glory.

We offer our prayers through Christ, that we may be always thankful for his mercy to us.

PROPER 24

Let us pray to God, the almighty and righteous Judge of the Church and the world.

Preserve your Church from false teaching and keep her firm in the inheritance of faith . . . Fill your ministers with zeal to preach the Gospel at all times.

Guide those who administer justice, that they may be honest and merciful in all they do . . . Give wisdom to all legislators, that law may prevail for the common good.

We pray that the children of our own families and those of our friends and neighbours may be brought up in the knowledge of faith . . . Bless the teachers who serve the children of this community.

Have mercy on those who are caught in legislation and find no solution . . . Grant them swift and honest judgement and release from their anxiety.

We pray that those who have died may be judged with mercy through the merits of Christ . . . May the Church on earth and in heaven be united in endless prayer and praise.

We make our prayers through Christ, whose judgement is ever merciful.

PROPER 25

Let us pray to the Lord, who casts down the proud and exalts the humble.

Preserve the Church from false pride . . . Teach us all to value our calling as by grace and not of our own goodness . . . May your word be made fully known through the preaching of your chosen ministers.

In a world where people put their trust in themselves and their own works, bring us the humility that is the only offering acceptable to you . . . Give the joy of human fellowship to those who in pride set themselves apart from others.

Strengthen us in service to you and to one another . . . Make us open to all in our community, welcoming those whose lives are different from our own.

Have mercy on the outcasts of the world, who are despised for their social position or way of life . . . Comfort all who have been forsaken by those whom they trusted.

We give thanks for those who have fought the good fight and are now at rest . . . Grant them the crown of righteousness prepared for those who have loved you to the end. We pray through Christ for mercy on our sins and on all sinners.

OR BIBLE SUNDAY

As Year A, p. 49.

DEDICATION FESTIVAL

As Year A, p. 50.

ALL SAINTS' SUNDAY

As Year A, p. 51.

FOURTH SUNDAY BEFORE ADVENT

Let us pray to the Father, who sent the Son to seek and save the lost.

As we begin to prepare for the coming of Jesus in his Incarnation, teach us to remember that he will come again to be our judge, and make us ready to meet him . . . Fill your Church with the sincere repentance that does not trust in outward show.

Give to those in authority and to all who influence the lives of others the spirit of mercy towards the oppressed and unprotected . . . May those who control money matters be just and honourable in their dealings.

Bless us, our families and friends, with a burning desire to be close to Jesus and to know him better . . . Help us to be generous in giving to those in need.

Have mercy on those who have turned from evil ways and yet are not accepted back . . . Relieve the distress of all whose lives have been damaged by the extortion and dishonesty of others.

We pray for those who have died, that they may be found worthy of your Kingdom . . . When they are judged, grant them the mercy of Christ.

We pray that we may be made fit to receive Christ in our homes and in our hearts.

THIRD SUNDAY BEFORE ADVENT

Let us pray to God, the giver of all life in this world and in the world to come.

Strengthen your Church to hold fast to the traditions which she has received . . . Knowing that we are justified in Christ alone, may we remain faithful until his coming again.

Give freedom to those in this world who are constrained by false legalism that holds them back from fullness of life . . . Bring to all nations the understanding that your ways are not ours and that your love is unbounded.

Grant to us, our families and friends, the grace of good deeds offered not for our own merit but for love of you and of our neighbours . . . Make us faithful witnesses in our community.

Have mercy on the childless couples who earnestly desire children . . . Comfort widows and widowers and all who are bereaved.

We pray that the departed may indeed be children of the resurrection, raised to their new life by you, the God of the living . . . Fulfil in them the good hope that sustained them in this world.

That we may come to Christ with wisdom and understanding, we offer our prayers in his name.

SECOND SUNDAY BEFORE ADVENT

Let us pray to God for protection and guidance in all dangers and perplexities.

Grant to your Church stability and peace, that she may faithfully guard the treasure of this present time yet always remember that at last the things of this world will pass away . . . Keep all Christian people strong in faith, never weary in doing good.

Into a world where many exploit the labours of others, bring a new spirit of co-operation and mutual respect ... May there be less concern for material riches, and a vision of your greater purpose for all.

Bless us in our families with shared love and loyalty at all times ... Give us patience and wisdom in meeting neighbours and colleagues who are hostile to us ... Make us more considerate of others, and more appreciative of those who work for the good of this community.

We pray for the victims of disaster, for the regions of the world where there is famine and epidemic disease ... We pray too for those unjustly accused, who are in peril of suffering and death.

Have mercy on those who have died violently and unprepared ... Grant them peace and new life in your Kingdom where there is no more pain or suffering.

Trusting in the mighty power of God revealed in Christ, we offer our prayers through him.

CHRIST THE KING

Let us pray to the Lord for pardon and peace in the Church and in all the world.

Keep the Church strong under Christ her head, faithful to the inheritance of his sacrificial love ... Make your priests and ministers good shepherds of the flock entrusted to their care.

We pray for those who do evil things from ignorance of the truth ... Where nations and races are divided, may they be reconciled through the love of Christ.

Grant us loving wisdom towards all those who need our care ... Bless our children and the children of our friends and neighbours . . . Support with grace all who do caring work in our community.

Have mercy on all who are derided for their beliefs or their way of life . . . Save and relieve all who suffer under power that is abused in the name of law.

We pray for those who have repented and turned to Christ in the hour of death . . . Receive them in your love, to be with him in his Kingdom for ever.

We offer our prayers in the name of Christ, our King of glory.

Common of the Saints

THE BLESSED VIRGIN MARY

For patient love to heal the Church and the world, let us pray to the Lord.

Guide your Church to follow the example of the Blessed Virgin Mary in patience, humility and trust ... As we honour her for the sake of her beloved Son, grant that we may know and make known the gentle love that he knew in his human family.

Teach our humanity to honour its wholeness in both male and female ... Bless the women who work for peace and justice, in organised movements or as lonely individuals ... Bring kindness and compassion into the places torn by strife.

We pray for mothers, especially those known to us who are under strain of poverty or anxiety ... Bless the ministry of women in this church ... We pray for women who work with maternal care in this community.

Have mercy on women suffering from cruelty and indifference ... Women in societies which deny them equal rights ... Those despised and ill treated by their families.

We join with the Blessed Virgin Mary in intercession for the departed ... In the hour of death, save us by the love of Christ which has raised them to eternal life.

We pray in the name of Christ, rejoicing in the grace given to his blessed Mother.

APOSTLES

Let us pray to God, who has given us sure knowledge of his unchanging truth.

As you have founded the Church on the teaching of the Apostles, grant that she may faithfully hold and make known the traditions which they taught . . . Give to all Christian people grace in their time to follow the example of your Apostle N whom we commemorate today.

May the light of the Resurrection faith shine in the world where vision is limited and hope is faint . . . Where races and nations fall apart in dissension, make them secure on the firm foundation of your love.

Keep us, our families and friends, constant in faith . . . Protect us from error and make us messengers of the good news to those with whom with live and work.

Have mercy on those who have been led astray by false doctrine and restore them to purity of faith . . . Release those who by seeking forbidden knowledge have fallen into the power of evil.

We pray for the departed who kept the faith and are now at rest . . . May they rejoice in the fellowship of the Apostles whose teaching was their guide in this world.

We pray that Christ will grant us true following of his blessed Apostles.

EVANGELISTS

Let us pray to God, whose word has gone out through the Church to all the world.

Empower your Church always to proclaim the saving message of the Gospel ... May the Holy Spirit who inspired your evangelist *N* be our guide into all truth.

Open the way for the spread of the Gospel into places where people still live in ignorance of its message ... Bless those who work through translation and publishing to make the faith more widely known.

Grant that in our families, our friendships and all our living we may fulfil the teaching of the Gospel ... Bless our reading of scripture and lead us always into new paths of understanding.

Come to the aid of those who long for Bibles and cannot obtain them ... Comfort and relieve all who suffer for their work of distributing Bibles in hostile lands.

We give thanks for those whose lives in this world were led by the light of the Gospel ... May they who loved the word of truth rejoice for ever in the presence of the living Word.

Rejoicing in the eternal message of salvation, we offer our prayers in the name of Christ.

MARTYRS

Let us pray to God, whose love brings victory out of suffering and death.

May the Church always have courage to preach the Gospel without fear, after the example of blessed *N* who witnessed to the world and did not count the cost ... Grant to all Christian people perseverance in their calling and faithfulness to the truth that they have been taught.

Have mercy on a world where good is often met with evil and love with anger . . . Open the eyes of men and women everywhere, to see and follow the goodness around them . . . Bless those in authority and lead them into the way of peace.

Give us strength when faith is hard and brings us into conflict with others . . . Help us to witness by word and example to those among whom we live and work.

We pray for all who suffer persecution for the sake of the Gospel . . . For all whose faith has alienated them from those who should be close to them . . . Give them courage in their affliction and soften the hearts of their persecutors.

We give thanks for all who have faithfully witnessed to the truth in this world . . . We pray that those who have suffered for their faith may find rest and eternal life in the realm where all tears are wiped away and there is no more pain.

We pray through Christ that we may be strong in the faith that sustained his holy martyrs.

TEACHERS OF THE FAITH AND SPIRITUAL WRITERS

That the Church and the world may be filled with holy wisdom, let us pray to the Lord.

Strengthen the Church in the ministry of teaching, that your people may be ready always to give a reason for the faith that they profess . . . We give thanks for the work of N whose gifts were used in your service, and pray for grace to do our part in making known the faith of Christ.

Bless all who are called to guide others through teaching and writing ... Increase the opportunities for education in the many parts of the world where they are few ... Encourage and enable those who are working against difficulties to improve their skills to be used in the service of humanity.

Give us grace to impart our faith to our families and friends and to those with whom we work ... Help us to speak with conviction but with tact, regarding the needs of others ... Bless all in this community who work in education and training.

We pray for those whose lives are limited by ignorance ... Grant new beginning to those who have lost their early opportunities for education ... Give perseverance to all who are learning new skills.

We give thanks for those who, having worked to teach and enlighten others in this world, have come through death to fuller knowledge of your glory ... Grant them the peace that passes all understanding.

We pray that the gifts entrusted to us may be fully used in the service of Christ.

BISHOPS AND OTHER PASTORS

For guidance and protection, let us pray to the Lord.

Bless your Church with gifts of care and nurture, and strengthen those who are called to be spiritual leaders .. We give thanks for the example of N in leading people to you and guiding them in the faith, and pray that we may in our time be as shepherds of your flock.

Give grace and wisdom to all in authority, to use their power for the good of those whom they govern ...

Bless those whose influence is hidden from the world in their quiet guidance of others.

Where we may have power to guide and direct, give us grace to use it in your service ... Help us to care for our families and for all who need the help that we can offer ... Bless those in positions of authority in this community.

We pray for all who are in distress through following bad advice ... Have mercy on those whose lives lack direction and bring them the care they need to become whole and independent.

We give thanks for all who have worked to lead others into the way of truth and now rest from their labours ... Grant to us in this life spiritual guidance that will lead us to eternal life.

That we may discern the true way and follow as we are led, we pray in the name of Christ.

RELIGIOUS

Let us pray to God, who calls men and women to obedience in his service.

Endow the Church with the spirit of discipline, keeping her faithful in ordered worship and witness ... Bless all whose lives of work and prayer are lived under vows of obedience ... We give thanks for the example of N who was called to the religious life and pray for strength in our own devotion.

Have mercy on this unruly world, and bring order where there is confusion and lack of direction ... Give wisdom to rulers and lawgivers, keeping them constant in care for those committed to their authority

... Bless all religious communities, that they may be beacons of light in the darkness.

Grant us order and security in our families and all our relationships ... Help us to follow regular lives of prayer and to be temperate in all we do.

Have mercy on those who have broken the vows they once made and fallen away from any part of their Christian profession ... Give strength to religious orders who work for the relief of poverty and distress.

We give thanks for all whose lives in religion witnessed to your love in this world and have now passed to rest ... We pray for those who care for the dying, and ask that their prayers shall ease the way through death to eternal life.

We pray that the order of our lives may confess our faith in Christ.

MISSIONARIES

Let us pray to God, whose faith has gone out through the Church into the world.

Bless the missionary work of the Church in this and in other lands ... Keep your people from looking only to their own lives of faith and make them eager for the spread of the Gospel ... We give thanks for *N* who brought the faith to those who had not heard it, and pray that we too may be used in your service.

Give light to all places in the world where there is ignorance of the Gospel ... Bless all missionaries and those who support them ... Prosper their work and give them strength when the way is hard.

Fill us with the zeal of mission in our daily lives ... Enable us to witness among those we meet in work and recreation ... Give us speech that is unswerving in faith but sensitive to the needs of others and respectful of their sincerity.

Have mercy on all who suffer restriction and persecution as they work to bring the Gospel to others ... Strengthen new converts whose faith is severely tested ... Comfort those who have been separated from families and friends by their love of your word.

Be merciful to those who in this world did not accept the Christian faith, but lived according to the good that they knew and worshipped as they understood ... Accept all in them that was of the truth ... Grant them the fullness of your presence and life in Jesus Christ, who died to redeem all our humanity.

That we may be faithful missionaries for Christ, we make our prayers in his name.

ANY SAINT

Let us pray to God, whose saints have shown his glory in the Church and in the world.

Guide your Church to follow the example of blessed N and of all your saints through the ages, and in this generation to glorify your name with joyful praise and reverent worship ... May we ever remember that to be called to your service is to be called to holiness.

We pray for a spirit of service towards those in need ... Fill our lives with love for you and for your creatures ... Sanctify all human striving towards a better world, that all may work together for good.

In all our relationships, grant us such love and grace that our discipleship shall be made plain ... Take away false showing and self-regard, to enable us to share our faith with those with whom we share our lives.

Have mercy on those whose goodness is exploited and whose innocence is abused . . . Be close to those whose lives have been damaged because they stood firm for truth and goodness . . . Give them strength to continue following those who have been your chosen witnesses.

We give thanks for all who have glorified you by their lives on earth and left us a good example, remembering especially blessed N . . . Give us grace to praise the memory of the saints not in words alone, but in lives that may make us worthy to share with them in your everlasting glory.

Knowing that we too are called to be saints, we pray for sanctification through Christ.

Special Occasions

NEW YEAR: NAMING AND CIRCUMCISION OF JESUS

That all things made be made new by his grace, let us pray to the Lord.

Direct and strengthen the Church, in which we are your children by adoption ... Send your people forward into this new year, bearing the name of Jesus for the salvation of all.

In the year that lies before us, grant peace in all places of strife ... Inspire with wisdom and mercy those who bear authority, that justice may prevail and wrongs be righted ... May your love shine graciously on all the world.

We pray for our families, friends and neighbours, that this year may be one of peace and blessing ... Shield with your loving care all babies and young children in this community and guide those who care for them.

Have mercy on all who face the future without hope ... At this time draw near with comfort to those who suffer in body, mind or spirit ... Give them new confidence in the name of Jesus.

We give thanks for all who, having confessed the name of Jesus in this world, are now at peace ... Grant them life eternal in the kingdom where there are no beginnings or endings but all is held in one perfection of being.

We make our prayers in the name of Jesus Christ, the Name above all names.

MOTHERING SUNDAY

Let us pray to God, who loves all people as a mother loves her children.

We give thanks for the example of Mary, mother of Jesus . . . We pray that our spiritual mother the Church may follow her in humility, trust and love.

Soften with a mother's gentleness all the hardness of human hearts . . . May the Holy Family of Nazareth bring blessing wherever people live together . . . Draw all races and nations to be one family in your love.

We pray for all mothers, especially those in our own and our local families . . . Give them the unfailing love that Mary gave to Jesus, and uphold them in times of anxiety and distress.

Have mercy on mothers who suffer for themselves or for their children, through sickness, misfortune or human cruelty . . . Give them the strength of your presence which comforted Mary in her sorrow.

Because your love is more constant than the love of any human mother, we pray with confidence for the repose of all who have died in the faith of Jesus Christ, Son of Mary and Son of God.

Seeking to have faith as little children, we offer our prayers through Christ our Lord.

THE GUIDANCE OF THE HOLY SPIRIT

In the power of the Holy Spirit, let us pray for the Church and for the world.

May the Holy Spirit lead the Church into all truth and keep her faithful to her calling . . . Grant to your people a right judgement in all things and the strength to follow where you will lead them.

Come with power into the world, to correct all false judgements that lead the nations into error ... Enlighten those in authority with clear vision, to use their power rightly for the good of all.

Bless us when we have difficult decisions to make ... Keep us, our families, friends and neighbours, in the right way ... Be with us in our work and shield us from error.

We pray for all who are led astray by false teaching or the lure of material gain ... Restore to them the light that has been darkened ... Change the hearts of those who pervert the ways of truth and justice.

We pray for those who have passed through this world and now rest where there is no more error and the darkness has passed away ... Grant them the fullness of life which they glimpsed here through the guidance of the Holy Spirit.

May all our prayers be truly offered in the spirit of Christ.

ROGATION DAYS

Let us pray in confidence to God who gives us power to pray.

Strengthen your Church to be constant in prayer, offering the acceptable worship to which we are called ... Unite all Christian people in the fellowship of prayer, knowing that what we ask in the name of Christ will be answered in the way that fulfils your divine purpose.

Hear the prayers that are sincerely offered across the world, supplying in grace what is lacking through human ignorance ... Grant a wiser use of the resources of your creation and bless those who work for their improvement.

Bless us in our prayers, to ask those things which are right for us and for those we love ... Help us to worship you in our families and in the company of all who are close to us in faith and love.

Have mercy on all who in despair and bitterness have lost their faith and ceased to pray ... Create again in them the love that they once had, and in their weakness restore to them the joy of your saving power.

We give thanks for the departed who knew you through prayer in this world and are now at rest ... Unite our prayers with those that they offer in the greater light of your presence, that the whole Church, seen and unseen, may be one.

As Christ has taught us to pray, we offer our prayers in his name.

THANKSGIVING FOR HOLY COMMUNION

Let us pray with thanksgiving to God, the giver of our spiritual food and of all grace.

Grant to your Church the continual grace of the sacraments ... Keep all Christian people faithful to your command of remembrance, recalling the price of our redemption and the source of our life ... Teach us to serve you in others, bringing to them the bread of life and the message of salvation.

Give to all nations hunger and thirst for righteousness through your living word ... Make all men and women understand the fellowship which they share in their common humanity, so that all life becomes a sacrament of your presence.

In the strength of the holy communion, send us out to make your power known to our friends and neighbours and colleagues ... Supply us with our bodily needs, and with the spiritual food and drink that makes us one with Christ.

We pray for all who are starving in the midst of plenty ... Bring new hope for the relief of their suffering ... Move the hearts of the rich and powerful to relieve the poor and weak.

We give thanks for all who have died sustained by the comfort of holy communion ... May they rejoice for ever in the heavenly banquet where the forms of bread and wine give way to the full revelation of Christ.

We offer our prayers, rejoicing in the communion that unites us with Christ.

HARVEST

Let us pray to God, the Lord of the harvest in all things material and spiritual.

As you have blessed the Church with abundant grace, keep her faithful in the offering of word and sacrament, knowing that all things come from you and return to you ... Send out your labourers to gather the harvest of the world, that all may know the riches of your love.

We pray for all who work that others may be fed, for those who bring in the harvest of the land and the sea ... We pray for those employed in the processing and transport of food . . . Grant a more just distribution of the goods of the world.

Give to us, our families and friends, grateful hearts for all your bounty and a concern for the needs of others . . . Bless those who work to bring meals to the poor and infirm in this community.

We pray for all who are hungry and undernourished . . . We pray especially for the children whose health is damaged by lack of food . . . Bless those who work for the relief of famine.

We give thanks for the departed who have been gathered into your care . . . Grant them the joy of faith brought to fruition in your heavenly Kingdom.

We offer our prayers, desiring to be faithful labourers for the harvest of Christ's Kingdom.

COMMEMORATION OF THE FAITHFUL DEPARTED

Let us pray to God, the Lord of all the living and the departed.

Keep your Church on earth ever mindful that she is one with the Church in heaven . . . Unite her prayers with the prayers of those who stand in your nearer presence . . . Fill all Christian people with zeal to continue the good work begun by the faithful in past ages.

In all striving and planning for the future, give to men and women grace not to forget the wisdom of the past . . . Let all acknowledge their human heritage, to guide them towards a future where your purposes shall be fulfilled.

We give thanks for all those we have loved and see no more, and for our families in past times before our knowledge ... We remember all who have helped us by word or example, and pray that we may in our time be good influences on those with whom we share our lives.

Be close to those who mourn the death of any whom they have loved ... Give them the comfort of human care, and the strength of your presence to continue their lives ... Bless them with faith in the resurrection of the dead to the life which holds no sorrow of parting.

We commit to your gracious keeping those who, having passed their brief time in this world, have returned to you, the Giver of life ... Deal mercifully with them, looking not upon their sins but upon the loving face of your Son Jesus Christ who died and conquered death ... Grant to us who remain the grace to die trusting in the same love.

Confessing our mortal weakness we pray to receive eternal life in Christ.

THE PEACE OF THE WORLD

Let us pray to God, the only Giver of peace to the Church and to the world.

Make your Church an instrument of peace, teaching by word and example the way of reconciliation ... Bless those who are working in areas of conflict to bring people together in the name of Christ.

Bring peace to all the places of strife and violence ... Fill the hearts of those in authority with the true love of peace and the desire to work for harmony with those who seem to be their enemies ... Bless the organisations that seek peace between nations.

Give us peace in our homes, with our neighbours and in our places of work . . . Inspire us with the love for others which may spread through them to heal the wider problems of the world.

Have mercy on the victims of war, the wounded, the refugees, those who have lost everything they had . . . Be with those who have no more hope and restore them to the fullness of life that is in you.

We pray for all who have died in war . . . Grant mercy to those who died unprepared and impenitent, through the love of Jesus who died by human cruelty . . . Give them the peace which they were denied in their last hour.

We make our prayers in the name of Christ, who has left his peace to his faithful people.

SOCIAL JUSTICE AND RESPONSIBILITY

Let us pray to the Father, the Lord of justice over all the earth.

Strengthen your Church to be a power for good in the relief of distress and in working for a better society . . . Save your people from being conformed to the false values of the world . . . Give them compassion and the will to work for justice.

Bless those in authority with the spirit of justice . . . Bring new life wherever inequality separates people from each other and keeps them from enjoying the fullness of life.

Help us to act fairly and honestly towards all those with whom we live and work . . . Be with those who work for the good of others in this community . . .

Bless them with your presence, giving them skill and compassion in their task of caring.

We pray for all who suffer from injustice in their lives and in their work ... Have mercy on all who are rejected by society and have no one to help them ... Visit and relieve with new hope those who have fallen into despair at their condition.

We pray for all who have died alone and unloved ... Receive them into the peace that they did not know on earth ... Because your mercy is everlasting and your love infinite, grant new life to those who have been driven by despair to end their own lives.

We pray in the name of Christ, who judges with mercy those who acknowledge their sin.

THE UNITY OF THE CHURCH

Let us pray to the Father, whose love draws all things in heaven and earth into one.

Grant to all Christian people the mutual love which is the duty of those called to be your own ... Strengthen our respect for those who acknowledge Christ in ways different from ours, and draw us towards the unity that is your will.

Bring the whole world closer to you in desire for peace and better understanding ... Take away prejudices which condemn any of your human family ... Teach people to seek fulfilment not in selfish interests but in the service of others.

Make us witnesses to our faith in harmony with our families, friends and neighbours ... Draw together those in this community who are separated from others and give them the desire to work for the good of all.

We pray for those who feel cut off from human fellowship because of their race or colour or way of life . . . Grant them the assurance of their worth and give to those who have rejected them the grace to seek and welcome them in love.

We give thanks for those who have lived the life of faith on earth and now are gathered into the eternal unity of the Church in Heaven . . . Rejoicing in their fellowship, may we learn to rejoice with one another.

We ask that our prayers may be united with the prayers of all who confess the faith of Christ.

MISSION AND EVANGELISM

Let us pray to God, the Lord of all races and nations.

Grant to your Church the power of the Father, the saving love of the Son and the guidance of the Holy Spirit, to preach the Gospel to all nations as you have commanded . . . Give to all Christian people the wisdom to meet others in their need and to bring them to you.

Take the ways and thoughts of this present age, correct what is wrong in them and convert them to your loving purpose . . . Give grace to all who are working for the spread of the Gospel.

Make your word known where it is lacking among any with whom we share our lives . . . Draw all who live and work in this community into the faith in which is the only true joy, now and for ever.

Come in power to those who have not heard the message of salvation . . . Give light to those who are in darkness and ignorance ... Turn the hearts of those who resist your love through indifference, pride or false assurance of their own strength.

Grant rest and peace to all who have laboured to make your word known ... Have mercy on those who have died without faith ... Through the love which created them though they did not understand, grant them now to know you as Lord and to enter into that holy fellowship which they did not find in this world.

In the name of Christ, we pray for grace to spread his good news which we have received.

MINISTRY, INCLUDING THE EMBER DAYS

Let us pray to God, who calls men and women to his service.

Confirm the Church in her continuing ministry to the world ... Raise up a devout fellowship, in which clergy and laypeople may work together for the Gospel ... Bless all who are preparing for ordination or for any special service in the Church.

Guide all people to discover the special calling that is your will for each of them ... Bless those who minister to the needs of others and give them light to know that all good works are empowered by you alone.

Grant that we may faithfully minister to all who are part of our care, to our families and friends, our neighbours and colleagues ... Awaken any in this community who have a vocation that they have not yet discerned.

Have mercy on all who feel the frustration of a calling unfulfilled ... Give them new hope, and open to them other ways of service . . . Visit and revive clergy and lay workers who have lost the joy they once knew.

We give thanks for all who have died after a life of service in Christian ministry . . . Grant them rest from their labours and eternal life in your presence.

That we may be eager in the service of Christ, we offer our prayers through him.

IN TIMES OF TROUBLE

Let us pray to God, whose compassion never fails and whose love is everlasting.

Keep the Church faithful when troubles come . . . Give your people courage to ask not for freedom from suffering but for strength to endure . . . Help us to care for others and to comfort their distress by the grace that reveals the mystery of love through suffering.

Have pity on the troubles of the world, through war and violence, through human sin and natural disasters . . . Give to all men and women true compassion for suffering and the will to work for its relief.

Grant that in our love for those near to us, we shall never forget the distress of others . . . Help us to use for good the gifts that you have given . . . Come with your healing power to any in this community who are in particular need at this time.

We pray for all who are afflicted . . . Heal the sick in body or mind and those who are weary with long illness . . . Comfort those who are sorrowful . . . When we do not know how to help others, accept our silent care for them and our trust in your mercy.

We pray for the departed whose dying has been hard and full of suffering . . . Grant them the wholeness of eternal life, where all tears are wiped away and there is no more pain.

We pray in the name of Christ for patience and hope in all our troubles.

FOR THE SOVEREIGN

Let us pray to God, the King of kings and Lord of lords.

Grant that your Church may live in peace with lawful authority, remembering that all true power comes from you alone . . . Give grace to Elizabeth our Queen and to all Christian rulers, that they may serve you in holiness of life.

We pray for those in authority, especially Elizabeth our Queen and all who serve under her . . . Grant them wisdom and right judgement and fill their hearts with a sincere desire for peace . . . May the power of this world be directed always towards the common good.

We pray for the royal family and all who work with them . . . Bless our own families, that they may be obedient to your commandments.

Have mercy on all who suffer from the abuse of power . . . Visit and relieve the victims of injustice, in great things or in small, and bring repentance to those who wrong them.

We give thanks for those who have ruled justly in this world and are now at rest . . . Grant to them and to all the departed eternal life in the Kingdom where all are equal and you reign as Lord.

We pray that we may be faithful citizens of this kingdom and of the Kingdom of Christ.

Afterword –
On Leading Intercessions

In most churches today laypeople are invited to lead the intercessions during the Eucharist. It is a responsibility which should be shared as widely as possible. All the Churches have rediscovered the importance of the laity in public worship. They are not simply those who have not been ordained to clerical ministry but the *laos*, the people of God who make up by far the largest order in his Church. A member of the clergy who leads intercessions speaks at that time for the whole Church rather than in the exercise of a special function as at other points in the service.

Here are a few suggestions to aid the intercessor: certainly not ten commandments, but ten points which are worth addressing for this solemn but most joyful ministry.

1 Read the scripture passages for the day. There is sure to be a copy of the lectionary in the church, but it is useful to have a personal copy if you are often called upon for intercessions. Pray for guidance as you prepare for this act of worship.

2 Write down what you want to say, fully or in notes according to your confidence in your own memory. If you use this book it may be best to copy out the words for the day, inserting any special needs in the appropriate places so that everything flows smoothly.

3 Make your intercessions particular by supplementing the suggested forms with specific immediate matters, local or from the wider world. Consult with your priest or minister about cases

of sickness or other trouble, or recent deaths. Respect confidentiality: sometimes people do not want their problems mentioned publicly.

4 Do not make your intercessions too particular. This is not the time for giving out the weekly notices, and God does not need all the details. Pray for 'the next meeting of the Parochial Church Council' rather than for 'the meeting of the Parochial Church Council which will be held in the vestry at 8 on Wednesday evening'; but it may be good to mention any special matter to be discussed. Do not try to read out all the names of members in a group or committee if they are numerous; apart from being tedious, it is easy to cause offence by forgetting someone.

5 Avoid voicing personal opinions. By all means pray for causes or groups which you have at heart, but do not extol their virtues or the wickedness of their opponents. We are all sinners and all children of God who loves us, and the oppressors need our prayers as much as the oppressed.

6 As well as careful reading of the scripture passages, consider whether there is a particular theme for the service. The idea of a weekly theme is not incorporated in the new lectionary, but it is wise to have a word with the preacher and see if there is anything that he or she would like picked up in the intercessions.

7 Do not take too long. Very long intercessions can lose the devout attention of the congregation and upset the balance of the service. As a very rough guide, double the length of the passages offered in this book should be the maximum. If these seem sufficient in themselves, with perhaps a few specific names, there is no need to run on further.

8 Be sure that your speech is clear and audible. Any of the clergy, or a trained lay reader, can help

here. Success comes from clarity and good projection, not shouting. Test the acoustics of the church from the place where you will be standing: even competent and experienced speakers can be caught out by a difficult building.

9   Use your natural voice, adapted only as necessary for being heard by more people. The affected 'parsonical' voice is, happily, almost extinct and needs no lay revival.

10 Despite all these injunctions, accept the duty with confidence and joy. Be reverent, but not anxious. You are offering prayer to a loving Father, in the presence of other Christians. This is, in the most wonderful sense, a family occasion.